# AMERICAN

# HERITAGE

*April 1960 · Volume XI, Number 3*

*Some railroads have commuter troubles and want subsidies; others have managed to survive. The oldest railroad in California is the Arcata and Mad River, often known as the "Annie and Mary." Founded in 1854 as the Union Plank Walk, Rail Track, and Wharf Company, it originally had redwood rails; locomotive power was provided by an old white horse named Spanking Fury. By the 1870's, business had become too much for the horse, and the company secured two engines, one of which is shown above on the Arcata wharf, Mr. V. Zaruba at the throttle. Under full steam, it could develop three horsepower, and must have given its engineer the same feeling of élan that comes to the driver of a small and dashing foreign car today. Our picture was taken in about 1897 by William Augustus Ericson, a pioneer photographer of lumbering and mining, 350 of whose plates were discovered by Lynwood Carranco during his research for a book about the Humboldt Bay country.*

# AMERICAN HERITAGE

*The Magazine of History*

PUBLISHER
James Parton
EDITORIAL DIRECTOR
Joseph J. Thorndike, Jr.
SENIOR EDITOR
Bruce Catton

EDITOR
Oliver Jensen
EXECUTIVE EDITOR
Eric Larrabee
ASSOCIATE EDITORS
Richard M. Ketchum
Joan Paterson Mills
Robert L. Reynolds
ASSISTANT EDITORS
Helen M. Brown, Robert Cowley
Stephen W. Sears
LIBRARIAN
Caroline Backlund
COPY EDITOR
Beverly Hill
ASSISTANT: Naomi S. Weber

ART DIRECTOR
Irwin Glusker
ASSOCIATE ART DIRECTOR: Murray Belsky
STAFF PHOTOGRAPHER: Herbert Loebel

ADVISORY BOARD
Allan Nevins, *Chairman*
Ray A. Billington       Alvin M. Josephy, Jr.
Carl Carmer            Richard P. McCormick
Albert B. Corey        Harry Shaw Newman
Christopher Crittenden  Howard H. Peckham
Marshall B. Davidson            S. K. Stevens
Louis C. Jones         Arthur M. Schlesinger, Sr.

CIRCULATION DIRECTOR
Richard V. Benson

AMERICAN HERITAGE is published every two months by American Heritage Publishing Co., Inc., 551 Fifth Avenue, New York 17, N. Y.
Single Copies: $3.95
Annual Subscriptions: $15.00 in U.S. & Canada
$16.00 elsewhere

An annual Index of AMERICAN HERITAGE is published every February, priced at $1.00. A five-year Cumulative Index of Volumes VI–X is available at $3.00.

AMERICAN HERITAGE will consider but assumes no responsibility for unsolicited material.

Title registered U.S. Patent Office.
Second class postage paid at New York, N. Y.

*Sponsored by*

American Association for State & Local History · Society of American Historians

## CONTENTS April 1960 · Volume XI, Number 3

COVER: Sunday afternoons were once a problem. What could a well-brought-up young lady do but paint china or read bound volumes of *Harper's Young People?* In the 1890's there was also something called the "card craze." Trade cards, chromolithographed and embossed, could be mounted in scrapbooks; and later on you could get pictures of brightly colored wildflowers, birds, and sentimental scenes to accompany them. Our seals of the first thirteen states come from just such a collection, now owned by the cartoonist Tomi Ungerer. *Back Cover:* Red Jacket, a chief of the Seneca Indians during post-Revolutionary days, was an orator as well as a warrior, and his Indian name meant "He Who Keeps Them Awake." He was an eloquent opponent of white civilization, despite the fact that he wears—in this painting from the Shelburne Museum, Shelburne, Vermont—a medal given him by George Washington.

# AMERICA AND RUSSIA: PART II

*By* ALLAN TEMKO

# RUSSIANS IN CALIFORNIA

4

Situated on a bleak Pacific headland, the reconstructed Fort Ross even today seems lonely and remote from civilization.

An Imperial colony on our

West Coast was their aim;

Fort Ross was their military

outpost; and the stakes—

higher than they realized

*Flag of the Russian-American Company*

On the swell of the morning tide, with all sails full, the *Juno* ran before the wind into San Francisco Bay. As the ship approached the Golden Gate, Fort San Joaquin—so unimposing that at first it seemed merely a group of rocks, rather than the main defense of the harbor— was sighted on the southern point. A "great commotion" within the fort, plainly visible from the ship, revealed the garrison's alarm at the unannounced arrival of a strange vessel. A soldier with a speaking trumpet hailed her in Spanish: "What ship is that?" For nearly half a century the Californians had been expecting the reply that now—at nine o'clock in the morning on April 8,

1806—they heard for the first time: "Russian."

The *Juno* was instructed immediately to cast anchor near the fort, under the guns of the battery. *"Sí, señor; sí, señor,"* answered the Russians, but they only simulated efforts to comply with the order. The ship continued swiftly into the deserted bay until she was out of range of the fort's battery. Then, prudently covering the beach with her own small cannon, she finally let go the anchor.

The appearance of the *Juno* in California culminated two hundred years of Russian expansion eastward from the Urals to the coasts of North America. Early in the sixteenth century, at the moment when English colonists were founding Virginia and Massachusetts, Cossack adventurers in search of sable and other furs swept across Siberia with a speed—and cruelty—unparalleled in the history of European conquest. By 1638, leaving behind them a wake of wanton slaughter, torture, and brutal exploitation of the natives, they reached the Sea of Okhotsk. Soon they were venturing out upon the Pacific, and before 1720 were at the Kuriles.

In 1741, after an earlier voyage in 1727–28 failed to touch the mainland, an expedition led by Vitus Bering, a Dane in the Czarist service, and the Russian Alexei Chirikov finally landed in North America. There the Russians soon made what was probably the greatest fur strike of all time, an almost incredible harvest of seal, blue fox, and sea otter pelts, which were marketed in China at extraordinary profit.

The rest of the world took notice; the long, relatively uneventful era of Hispanic supremacy in the Pacific was coming to an end. Spain, of course, although her massive and ornate imperial façade would not collapse until the next century, was especially apprehensive of the Russian presence in the northern ocean. For the vast and undefined province of Upper California, whose coast line alone had been explored, and that imperfectly, lay exposed to any intruder.

After 1750, when garbled reports of Bering's discoveries commenced to reach western Europe, intrusion by Russia seemed imminent. The Spanish embassy at St. Petersburg repeatedly warned Madrid of Russian ambitions in the New World; and the able Bourbon Charles III acted.

A vigorous official, José de Gálvez, was sent to New Spain as *visitador general,* and in 1769 he launched five "sacred expeditions" of leather-jacketed troops and Franciscan missionaries—two groups proceeding overland from Mexico through deserts and mountain ranges, and three by sea along the wind-buffeted coast —to establish Spanish settlements in California at last. That year the Mission and Presidio of San Diego were founded. The following spring a fort was erected at Monterey "to defend us from the atrocities of the Russians, who were about to invade us." But not until 1776, a week before the signing of the Declaration of Independence on the other side of the continent, did the occupation of San Francisco begin. For the moment the Spaniards could advance no farther northward. They spent the rest of the century completing the chain of nineteen missions—spaced roughly a day's journey apart along the coast—between San Diego and San Francisco.

Spain had acted none too quickly in California. By this time every maritime power—Britain, France, Holland, the United States—was alive to colonial and commercial possibilities in the Pacific. No one realized how high the stakes actually were, but the known stake in furs was high enough. Captain Cook's account of his famous voyage of 1778–79, in which he dwelled on the wealth of furs in Nootka Sound near what is now Vancouver Island, electrified Europe and America. English and Yankee vessels commenced taking pelts in northern waters. A French expedition under the Comte de La Pérouse reconnoitered the coast in 1786, and put in for ten days at Monterey.

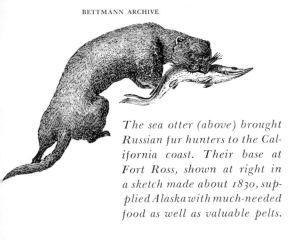

*The sea otter (above) brought Russian fur hunters to the California coast. Their base at Fort Ross, shown at right in a sketch made about 1830, supplied Alaska with much-needed food as well as valuable pelts.*

*Waning fortunes made the Russians give up Fort Ross in 1841; twenty-six years later they sold Alaska to the U.S. Posts like New Archangel (at left) fell into decay as the sea otter and northern fur seal (above) were hunted almost out of existence.*

The growing number of foreign vessels in the region increased Spain's suspicions. Measures were taken to seal California from the rest of the world. Trade was forbidden. Additional guns were mounted at the tiny presidios. But audacious Yankees poached furs along the sparsely settled coast, openly defying the Spaniards, who lacked ships to chastise them.

In the meantime, despite fierce native resistance, the Russians were consolidating their own position in the north. A station was set up on the island of Kodiak in 1784; and in 1799 headquarters were established at Sitka for the Russian-American Company, a fur monopoly whose interests went well beyond mere trade. Although Catherine the Great had renounced territorial aspirations in the New World, her mad son, Paul I, had given way to his courtiers, and granted the company a far-reaching charter. Now Paul's son—and perhaps his murderer—the young Alexander I, was Czar. At this stage of his reign Alexander gave signs of being a liberal ruler of the Western type; and he was surrounded by ministers whose ideas and methods —rational and efficient to a degree unprecedented in Russia—apparently also resembled those of the West. Most of these men of the new type, like their Czar, had ambitious plans for Russia. One of them, in fact, the Czar's Chamberlain, Nikolai Petrovich Rezanov,* stood on the *Juno*'s deck, coolly directing her when she ran past the guns of Fort San Joaquin, through the Golden Gate and into San Francisco Bay.

A curious train of circumstances brought the Grand Chamberlain of the Russian Empire to the remote Spanish outpost. Nearly three years earlier, on August 7, 1803, Rezanov had sailed from the Baltic as the senior dignitary of the first Russian expedition around the world. Two ships, the *Nadezhda* and the *Neva,*

* For another view of Rezanov, see George Howe's "The Voyage of Nor'west John," in the April, 1959, AMERICAN HERITAGE.

made the journey. Officially the Chamberlain's title for this mission was Plenipotentiary and Envoy Extraordinary to the Emperor of Japan, but his broad discretionary powers extended to the entire Pacific.

At Nagasaki in the winter of 1804–05, however, Rezanov met with humiliation and failure when he sought a trade agreement with the xenophobic Japanese. Rezanov, a proud man, was furious, and intended to return immediately to St. Petersburg to request the Czar's permission to conduct a punitive expedition against Japan. But at Kamchatka in Siberia, he found letters ordering him to inspect the Alaskan holdings of the Russian-American Company.

Rezanov was admirably qualified to make this inspection tour. Few Russians were as familiar as he with their nation's interests in the Pacific; few had as great a personal stake in the struggle for power that was taking place on the American coast. For although he came from a family that had possessed noble status since the sixteenth century, Rezanov was a self-made man whose future was bound closely to the fate of Russian America. His hereditary title of *barin,* which is often mistranslated as "baron," signified only that he was a member of the minor nobility. He did well at court as a guards officer, but the turning point of his career was his marriage to a daughter of the principal founder of the Russian-American Company, Grigori Ivanovich Shelekhov. The girl's dowry consisted of a large block of shares in the company; and when she died in 1802, shortly after the birth of their second child, Rezanov became independently wealthy. With Shelekhov's widow, he directed the operations of the company, and he advanced brilliantly at the court of Alexander I. As protégé of the Czar's leading minister, Count Rumiantsev, he was named Chamberlain, Privy Councilor, and Procurator of the Senate. Yet, although Rezanov was only forty-one years old when he was or-

*Pierre Landais was a supercharged egoist of whom Benjamin Franklin wrote: "If . . . I had 20 ships of war at my disposition, I should not give one of them to Captain Landais."*

# THE REVOLUTION'S CAINE MUTINY

In Pierre Landais the Continental Navy had its own real-life Commander Queeg. His tour as master of the *Alliance* was a nightmare wilder than any a novelist could invent

*By* RICHARD B. MORRIS

In a prefatory note to *The Caine Mutiny* Herman Wouk makes the point of informing the reader that "the records of thirty years show no instance of a court-martial resulting from the relief of a captain at sea under Article 184, 185, and 186 of the Naval Regulations," and that both persons and events in his novel are imaginary. Had his researches carried him back much farther into the American past, as far back as the closing years of the American Revolution, he might have uncovered a singularly parallel case, one where fact proved even stranger than his fiction.

The mutiny on the Continental frigate *Alliance* occurred under much the same circumstances as on the mine sweeper *Caine*. In both cases the captains were relieved of command because they were considered by their officers to be no longer in control of their mental faculties. Lieutenant Commander Philip Queeg and Captain Pierre Landais were both martinets who threw tantrums over the slightest infraction of their orders. Both had paranoid personalities, were unreasonably suspicious and gripped by feelings of persecution, and both sought to withdraw from reality when the crisis came. Both were petty and arbitrary toward their subordinates, arguing with them over the ship's water and food supplies. And

finally, the reputations of both commanders were destroyed as a result of sensational courts-martial.

Congress christened one of the largest and best-built ships in the Continental Navy the *Alliance* and then fittingly gave command of the swift-sailing frigate to a Frenchman. He was a naval captain named Pierre Landais, a supercharged egoist whose conduct proved of great disservice to Franco-American amity.

From her maiden voyage, the *Alliance* seemed destined to ride stormy seas. In the winter of 1779 she sailed for France with Lafayette as a passenger. Hardly had she left Boston when Landais revealed what was to be a characteristic weakness as a disciplinarian. Writing to Franklin in February, 1779, Landais reported that he had reached Brest only after putting down a full-scale mutiny of the crew with the aid of the Marquis and the officers of the ship. As a result of a court of inquiry held on shipboard, thirty-eight of the crew were put in irons and on reaching port were confined to a French prison without the formality of a trial.

Benjamin Franklin, who directed American naval operations in foreign waters in addition to running interference for the Franco-American alliance, now ordered Landais and the *Alliance* to report to L'Orient and there join John Paul Jones's squadron. John

*The* Alliance *(right) passes Boston Light at the end of her mutiny-scarred voyage. To the Navy Board a distraught Landais reported: "I cannot even trust my clerk . . ." The picture was painted by Matthew Parke, the frigate's captain of Marines.*

Adams, who had been in France as a commissioner, was now anxious to return home on the *Alliance,* and during this period spent a good deal of time in Landais' company. Adams found him frustrated in his ambitions, disappointed in love, unable to win the affection of his officers or hold their respect, and consumed by jealousy. In his diary for May 12, 1779, Adams recorded: "Landais is jealous of everything, jealous of everybody, of all his officers, all his passengers; he knows not how to treat his officers, nor his passengers, nor anybody else." He found him a bewildered man, constantly harping on imaginary plots against him. Adams, who served as peacemaker between captain and crew, predicted that when he left the ship "all will become unhappy again." He entered a further prediction: "Landais will never accomplish any great thing . . . This man . . . has a littleness in his mien and air. His face is small and sharp so that you form a mean opinion of him from the first sign."

It did not take Landais long to confirm Adams' prognosis. His astounding behavior during the notable engagement of the *Bonhomme Richard* and the *Serapis,* which took place in the North Sea on September 23, 1779, only seven months after the *Alliance* arrived in European waters, should have been conclusive evidence that he was dangerously unstable. With the converted Indiaman and the more heavily gunned British frigate both afire, Jones was relieved when the *Alliance* finally made her appearance. To his consternation his would-be rescuer discharged a broadside into the stern of the *Bonhomme Richard.*

"For God's sake forbear firing into the *Bonhomme Richard!*" Jones shouted frantically, but Landais continued to pour shot into Jones's ship. One of his volleys killed several men and an officer of the forecastle, and others hit the *Bonhomme Richard* under water. Only fantastic bravado saved the day for Jones.

"Either Captain Landais or myself is highly criminal, and one or the other must be punished," Jones complained to Franklin. But the political climate made it imprudent to take such action in France against a French officer, even though he held an American commission, and Franklin referred the issue to the Continental Congress. Whether Landais acted from treachery or made an incredible blunder cannot now be determined. Suffice it to report that the Frenchman was not cashiered from the service at that time. What is more, he had the effrontery to insist that Jones return to him the command of the *Alliance,* which Franklin had turned over to the peppery Scot. And here the intrigues and feuds among the American commissioners in France—Franklin, Arthur Lee, and Silas Deane—played right into Landais' hands.

Despite the patent evidence of his instability, incompetence, and possible treachery, Landais was supported in his claim to the command of the *Alliance* by the quarrelsome and suspicious Lee, a born troublemaker who had a running feud with Deane and Franklin. Out of perversity he encouraged Landais to recover the command of the *Alliance.* Lee notified Jones that Franklin was without authority to divest Landais of the command of the frigate that Congress had conferred upon the Frenchman. Warning Jones against "a rash and illegal action," Lee, in a typically self-righteous vein, insisted that his duty to his country and his "love of law and order" impelled him to stop Jones from interfering. John Adams, who took a dim view of his Paris colleagues, later backed up Lee, despite his private reservations about Landais' character.

Encouraged by Arthur Lee and animated by a consuming envy of Paul Jones, Landais plotted to get the *Alliance* back. On June 13, learning that Jones had gone ashore, he boarded the ship in L'Orient Harbor at a time when virtually all the officers who had previously served under him were on the quarterdeck and all Jones's officers were below at dinner. He was greeted with loud huzzas. Jones's officers were summoned on deck, Landais' commission from Congress was read to them, and all officers of the late *Bonhomme Richard,* as well as all others who did not acknowledge his authority, were summarily ordered ashore. Landais would not allow any of the crew to leave, however. Jones's men were kept in the hold in irons. The rest seemed happy at the coup, as they were dissatisfied by Jones's delay in distributing their share of the prizes gathered in recent encounters. A notorious martinet himself, Jones was scarcely beloved by his seamen.

When Jones learned how he had been outwitted, he was beside himself. Midshipman Nathaniel Fanning, a loyal Jones supporter, tells us that "his passion knew no bounds; and in the first paroxysm of his rage he acted more like a madman than a conqueror." But once he regained command of himself, Jones, though normally not distinguished for his prudence, began to behave with surprising circumspection. Instead of confronting Landais and reasserting his rights at once, he chose to run off to Paris to obtain authorization from the American and French governments. Franklin provided him with written instructions explicitly ordering Landais to quit the ship immediately. M. de Sartine, the French minister of marine, issued a warrant in the king's name for Landais' arrest.

Meantime the crafty Landais was by no means idle. When Jones returned from Paris on June 20, he found that the *Alliance* had been moved from L'Orient to nearby Port Louis. Presenting his two orders, Jones called upon the captain of the port, his friend Antoine Thévenard, for help. Among the papers in the Naval Manuscripts Collection of the Franklin D. Roosevelt Library is an order by the port officials for the disposition of ships and men to prevent the escape of the *Alliance*. A boom was promptly moved across the harbor to block Landais' exit, and a gunboat armed with three 24-pounders and manned by sixty-five men was ordered to stand by to prevent the boom from being cut. Orders were given to the commander of the citadel to fire on the frigate if she attempted to pass. To take the *Alliance,* Jones was provided with a small flotilla of three warships, along with their armed boats, one hundred soldiers from the garrison, and one hundred marines.

For reasons of prudence or delicacy, Jones abstained from accompanying the expedition. When Landais was called upon to yield the frigate, he replied: "If you come within reach of my cannons I will sink you." That was enough for the task force. They turned tail and returned to port. And that, surprisingly, was enough for John Paul Jones, too. For some reason he suddenly got cold feet. He had the order to fire upon the *Alliance* reversed and the boom removed. He justified his strange *volte-face* in a letter to Robert Morris written on June 27: "My humanity would not suffer me to remain a silent witness of bloodshed between allied subjects of France and America," he declared. Jones accused the officers of the port of acting "rather like women than men," but his own indecision and his failure to accompany the expedition reveal him in this episode to have been a bumbler rather than a hero.

The boom removed, Landais slipped out to sea on the eighth of July. Trouble was not slow to appear. At least one officer aboard the *Alliance* did not take enthusiastically to Landais' seizure of power. He was Captain Matthew Parke, in charge of the marines, who had received his orders from Jones. Parke had agreed to defend the ship and "her commander," but the other officers were to defend themselves. Landais

*The* Alliance *flew the flag at top and the vanquished* Serapis *the one at bottom as they sailed into a Dutch port after the* Bonhomme Richard's *pyrrhic victory in 1779.*

regarded this as a reflection upon his authority and ordered the purser, Nathaniel Blodget, to keep near Captain Parke and if he "saw any treachery in him to run him through the body." Blodget considered this an "extraordinary" order and told Landais flatly he would not obey it. But Landais was taking no chances. On June 21, while still in Port Louis, he had Parke arrested, only to release him once the ship was at sea. It was his first serious blunder of the voyage.

The recapture of the command brought Landais little peace of mind. His behavior was agitated; he grew fretful and slept very little (and that in the daytime); he was distrustful of his own officers, and as his purser later testified, "gave his friends a good deal of pain." He was constantly creating new difficulties and stirring up imaginary ones. Nobody aboard ship was exempt from his tyrannical moods, not even the five passengers, most prominent among them Landais' staunch supporter, Arthur Lee, who had taken along a private cargo of goods, at government expense, for his own profit. One day at the dinner table Lee complained that the officers and passengers were required to drink water from the filthy common scuttle cask. Landais retorted that the water was good enough for the captain and that they ought to be content even though the water stank. By now thoroughly enraged, Landais brandished the carving knife and slammed it down on Lee's fork as the celebrated passenger was trying to help himself from the common dish. "I'll let you know I am captain of the ship," he cried, "and I shall be helped first at the table. You shall not pick the liver out of the dish. You shall take the first piece that comes to hand as I do."

That volley seemed to confound Lee.

"What do you mean? I don't ever remember disputing you being the captain of the ship. I was never so used in my life," he expostulated.

"When you get ashore," said Landais, "you may load your pistols as soon as you please."

Landais' gluttony and his eccentricities kept the ship in a constant turmoil. He got into a man-size row with his officers. Before leaving Boston for France on

CONTINUED ON PAGE 88

13

*Fanny Knight, with her luminous dark eyes and shoulder-length curls, was fourteen and just emerging into womanhood when she sat for this portrait, two years before leaving on her Grand Tour. This picture and those of her mother and father on page 16 were painted by an unknown artist.*

# Miss Knight Abroad

For a provincial belle from Natchez, the Grand Tour was a priceless

introduction to Europe's art, its feudal pomp, and its tourist trade

*By* ALEXANDRA LEE LEVIN

For upper-class Americans of the 1850's the Grand Tour of Europe was at once the fulfillment of a lifelong ambition and a flamboyant way of letting their neighbors know that they had arrived. To lives made wealthy by the whirring wheels of northern industry or bumper harvests of southern cotton, they were anxious to add a patina of culture; the Grand Tour seemed the quickest and surest method of absorbing something which America lacked but which time-mossed Europe possessed in ample measure.

So *nouveau riche* Americans, with John Murray's guidebooks in hand, oh'd and ah'd their way around the British Isles and the Continent, stopping in Rome or Florence to have their portraits painted in oils, their profiles preserved in enduring marble, or their silhouettes struck in cameo. And when they came home again, their *objets d'art,* their Paris clothes, and their tales of adventure marked them as folk worthy of admiration and envy.

The summer of 1854 saw a typical family of American tourists, Mr. and Mrs. John Knight and their sixteen-year-old daughter Fanny, sail from New York on the fast steamer *Pacific* of the Collins Line. Mr. Knight, my great-grandfather, was a retired cotton merchant of Nat-

chez, Mississippi, who had worked hard for years; now he wished to spend his money seeking to restore his shattered health at foreign watering places and educating his attractive, dark-eyed daughter. Their tour was to last five years, and to take them to all of Europe's major cities—and even to the warm sands of Egypt.

Recently I came into possession of their great iron-bound trunk (below), passed down through the family and unopened since 1882. Inside, among many other mementos of the trip, was Fanny's lively diary. Her story—illustrated with passports, hotel bills, old prints, *cartes de visite,* and even a sonnet written to her by an amorous Italian—is told on the next fourteen pages, largely in Fanny's own words.

The diary begins with a note on June 24, 1854: "This day at 12 o'clock we bade farewell to the shores of my own dear America. How my bosom throbbed as I heard the cannon sounding from our boat and from other vessels around us, announcing our departure." Her mother became seasick almost immediately, "and Pa was just managing," but Fanny was having the time of her young life. To her intense delight she was on her way to becoming, in the literal sense of the words, a Woman of the World.

15

*Frances Knight*     *John Knight*

# *London... and the Queen*

During the twelve-day voyage to England Fanny Knight took a lively interest in her fellow passengers, among whom were a groom of sixty and his bride of twenty-one. "Strange to say," Fanny confided to her diary, "I never see them together." Also aboard were two young American girls en route to Spain to join a convent. One of them tried to persuade Fanny to go with them, but found her too much attached to the "sinful pleasures" of the world.

Sinful pleasures were scarce in Queen Victoria's London. Hiring a Bath chair, the Knights rode to suburban Sydenham, where the famed Crystal Palace built for the Great London Exhibition of 1851 had been reconstructed. There it stood in all its glass-and-metal glory, housing mawkish neoclassic sculpture, "curiosities" from far-flung and romantic places, and a bewildering array of objects in wood, metal, pottery, and heavy cut glass—all crowded together higgledy-piggledy. It bore the authentic stamp of Victorian England—a mixture of religiosity and worship of the machine, the Mammon of the age. The stamp impressed itself upon the soft wax of the Western world: the Knights were delighted with the Palace and the elaborate grounds.

But for young Fanny the high light of their visit to London was a glimpse of Victoria herself. "The Queen passed us on the street in her carriage today," she wrote. "She was on her way to the Duchess of Gloucester's to attend a juvenile ball with the children. Prince Albert rode beside her, and in front of her sat the Princess Royal Helena and the Prince of Wales, all looking very neat and modest. The Police seemed very proud of their Queen as she sat there in her pink silk bonnet. One of them said to Pa: 'She looks just like a little girl!' "

CORLISS
H & J. Ameri----- PACIFIC, ----- --

The Knights began their Grand Tour on the Collins Line's *Pacific* (left), which later disappeared at sea. A souvenir of their visit to the Crystal Palace was the chromolithograph (above) of part of the French exhibit— "tasteful and elegant" statuary, rug-work "having the effect of velvet," and "beautiful . . . decorative furniture." At right are letterheads —and a bill—from various English hotels and inns. In July, tea and strawberries cost two shillings in Brighton, and breakfast for three was only four shillings more.

# *Pageantry in Paris*

The next stop was Paris, where Fanny and her mother, after the fashion of American ladies then and now, shopped for gowns, gloves, and fripperies in lace. "Hoops are still in vogue," Fanny noted. "On the Champs-Élysées, the ladies occupy so much room in the carriages that it is as much as one can do to find out the poor gentlemen's heads, which are peeping out from the flounces which envelop them. The men always remind me of so many modest little daisies afraid to show their heads."

The capital was extremely gay. One Sunday morning Fanny arose to find all Paris preparing for a fete in honor of Emperor Louis Napoleon. The military was out, hand organs played in the streets, and great crowds surged along the boulevards. In the evening everything was a blaze of lights. The wily Louis was endeavoring to make the populace forget the bloody struggles of 1848, and he was succeeding admirably: already hundreds of buildings that had been reduced to rubble had risen again.

"The Emperor has a twofold design in view," Fanny wrote, "the embellishing of the city, and keeping the people out of mischief, for he well knows that his security lies in keeping the working class employed so that it will have no time to meditate revolution. We have seen the Emperor several times, as well as the Empress Eugénie. Louis Napoleon is a fine looking man—at least he appears that way in an open phaeton—is rather pallid and wears an immense moustache . . . He dresses plainly in a dark blue cloth suit with gilt buttons and a plain black hat. The Empress has the most beautiful neck and shoulders that I ever saw, and her bust is considered one of the finest."

Many years before, Louis Napoleon's uncle, Jérôme Bonaparte, had married a beautiful American girl, but his family had refused to recognize her. Now, as Jérôme passed them in the royal cavalcade, Mrs. Knight and her daughter indulged in a bit of chauvinism, mixed with womanly solidarity. "Ma remarked to me," Fanny wrote, "that Prince Jérôme looked rather superannuated although his wig is so black. It is hard to believe that this old man was once the dashing lover of Mistress Betsy Patterson in Baltimore!"

From Paris the Knights toured the Low Countries and visited the Field of Waterloo, where they encountered an enterprising British coach operator (see top left). Then, as winter neared, they turned southward along the path to Rome.

*In Brussels the Knights found the British, who had won the day at Waterloo, trying to win the battlefield tourist trade too, in coaches driven only by "steady English coachmen."*

Two of the many places the tourists visited in Paris were the Molière fountain (above) and the Chamber of Deputies (left). Louis Napoleon, with Empress Eugénie (below), made a shrewd bid for the people's loyalty, Fanny observed, by opening a Palace of Industry and by "imperial dashings about the city . . . which are colourful and eye-catching, and quite a contrast to the drabness of his predecessor, Louis-Philippe."

# A Winter in Italy

A large and cosmopolitan artists' colony flourished in Rome during the 1850's, and it was considered fashionable for visitors to the city to make the rounds of the studios, looking at works of art, admiring and criticizing, and often buying. Fanny and her parents visited almost fifty studios and were for the most part pleased with what they saw. But their interest in culture was kept firmly within the bounds of Victorian propriety. Mrs. Knight kept a travel diary, too, and to it she confided: ". . . we went to Mr. William Page's studio and saw two of his Venuses. They are entirely too nude, one being in a lying posture, the other standing on a dolphin. At the studio of John Gibson, an English sculptor, I did not care at all for his painted statue of Venus, as the pink colouring of the marble makes her look indecent."

The artist whom the Knights visited most often was young Edward Sheffield Bartholomew, a shy, lame sculptor from Hartford, Connecticut. Fanny and her mother "sat for their busts," and Mr. Bartholomew gallantly squired the ladies around Rome. They walked wondering through the baroque vastness of St. Peter's, and one evening after dinner, as Fanny was walking in the Piazza del Popolo, she saw the Pope himself—it was Pius IX—pass quite close to her. "He was attended by two Cardinals," she wrote, "while two heralds on horseback announced his approach. The cortege was very plain and unpretending, his carriage being the only object which had any pretensions to grandeur and style. The pope looked remarkably well and seemed pleased."

The tourists remained in Rome for some time—long enough to participate in the social life of the international colony. And in Rome, too, Fanny began acquiring some of the intellectual attainments which, in her father's mind, had been one of the purposes of their tour. She studied music and art, and took lessons in Italian from Signor Vincenzo Sanguinetti, a most attractive gentleman. The winter passed pleasantly in the warm Italian sun, but with the return of spring they would be off again. One evening Signor Sanguinetti called for a farewell visit. Bowing low over Fanny's hand, he placed in it a note (above, right), beautifully decorated with gilded cupids, bows and arrows, and a pink Venus reclining in a sea shell towed by swans. It was a sonnet he had written to the "lovely damsel" from Natchez—a romantic memento for young Fanny Knight as she headed south with her parents for Naples.

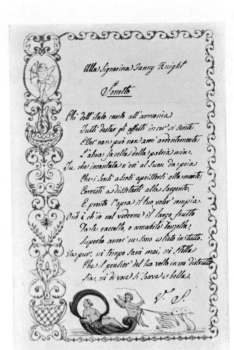

*The romantic sonnet above was Fanny's farewell present from her Italian teacher, the handsome and charming Signor Vincenzo Sanguinetti. After devoting eleven of his fourteen lines to praising the Italian language, he finally got around to Fanny in the last three:*

Now go: nor will there ever be a time
    or star
When the thought of your face will vanish from me,
Nor of your voice so sweet and beautiful.

*In Rome Fanny also went to a reception in honor of ex-President Millard Fillmore (below) and saw Pope Pius IX on his throne (above right). As spring came, the Knights left for Naples, with its spectacular volcano, Mt. Vesuvius (right).*

Among the many mementos which the Knights brought back from Europe were views of Venice (above) and Pompeii (left). Although Venice, at the time of their sojourn in Italy, was languishing under Austrian rule, it was about to enjoy a rebirth of popularity among artists, men of letters, and just plain tourists from all over the world. "A city of marble, did I say?" John Ruskin exclaimed. "Nay, rather a golden city, paved with emerald!" Their Italian tour took the Knights from the splendors of the Renaissance to the sophistication of the an-

cient Roman Empire. Among
the buildings of Pompeii
which could be seen in something like their condition at
the moment Vesuvius buried
the town, was the House of the
Tragic Poet (left), immortal-
ized two decades before in
Bulwer-Lytton's popular novel. One drawing found in
Fanny's trunk, however, was
the work of her own hand. It
was the view at right of a cha-
teau near Pau in the Pyrenees,
where she and her parents
wintered; there Fanny found
time to put to use the art train-
ing acquired in Rome. The
results were not at all bad.

# Tall Alps and Kremlin Towers

From France the tourists went to Switzerland and climbed one of the snow-capped Alps to the famous Hospice of St. Bernard. They visited the grisly "Dead House," where the bodies of travelers who had perished in the snow were ranged about the walls in the attitudes of their final agonies, uninterrable because of the hard, rocky ground and incorrupt in the cold, dry mountain air. Among the Knights' fellow guests was Senator Charles Sumner of Massachusetts, who the spring before had been caned in the Senate by Representative Preston Brooks of South Carolina. "I certainly do not think [Sumner] a flattering specimen of an American Senator," wrote Fanny, a loyal southerner. "I never justified Mr. Brooks in his conduct, and to say the least think he acted in a most ungentlemanly manner, but I do think Mr. Sumner deserved all he got." When she saw his signature in the guest register as "The Hon. Charles Sumner, Senator of the United States," it was more than Fanny could stand. "I think it in very bad taste," she wrote, "for an American in particular to be his own trumpeter."

Another winter in the Italian sunshine was followed by a trip to Russia, where Alexander II had ascended the throne in 1855. At St. Petersburg their luggage was searched and all their books taken away so a censor could examine them. In Moscow—which they reached via an American-built railroad—they visited the magnificent gold and white apartments of the empress in the Kremlin, watched droshky races, fireworks, singing gypsies, and a "Bear Woman," and went to a prison to see criminals and political prisoners leaving for Siberia. "It was a most heartrending scene," Fanny wrote. "The poor creatures looked pale and thin; they wore the prison garb and had their heads shaved with the exception of a small spike on the top. There were some women among them. Many kind persons were present who gave the exiles money, for without it they would certainly starve on the road to their inhospitable home. The prisoners were chained and hand-cuffed, and must go on foot all the way to Siberia where most of them will work in the mines for life. The parting of the prisoners from their families and friends was most distressing; their cries were heard until the order for the drums to beat was given, and the exiles proceeded on their journey. The prisoners shed not a tear; they seemed to have lost all emotions of any kind, just a numbness remained. Thank God I was born neither a serf nor a prince in this land!"

24

At the Alpine Hospice of St. Bernard (left)—reached via charabanc and mule-back—Mrs. Knight and Fanny, a bit uneasy at spending the night in a Catholic monastery, carefully looked under the beds and bolted the doors before retiring. The splendor of the Kremlin (above) and the luxurious homes of the Russian nobility greatly impressed young Fanny, though not enough to obscure the fact that the serf —and the dissenter—were not so well off.

# Up the Nile in Style

As another winter neared, Fanny's father was anxious to head south before his chronic asthma became troublesome. Egypt was then the Florida of the well to do, and boat trips up the Nile had become fashionable. At Cairo they found a dragoman who agreed to manage everything for the sum of £250. A boat, called the *Luxor,* was fitted out with furniture, beds and bedding (the sheets were to be changed once a week, the table linens twice), a coal stove, and provisions of the best quality. An American flag was run up at the stern, the captain and his crew of Nubians came aboard, and on February 17, 1859, the *Luxor* raised her sails to the breeze.

Along the way the boat stopped to allow the party to make side excursions—to the Temple of Karnak, the pyramid of Cheops, the falls at Aswan. Fanny and her parents rode in donkey chairs to various ruins, picking up archaeological souvenirs.

From Aswan they headed downstream again for Cairo. "The captain's wife," Fanny noted, "a rather good looking Nubian woman with pearly teeth, saw him off at Assuan, and wafted him a blessing by throwing dates into the water. The captain has a wife at Cairo, also, and another, his favorite, at Luxor. Abdul Wahee, the head cook, has had five wives, but has sent all but two away, as he is in the habit of doing after they reach the age of twenty-six." The *Luxor* reached Cairo on April 7 after covering 250 miles in a little over seven weeks.

Next stop was Alexandria, where Fanny dropped in at the Union Dispensary to order a bottle of honey of rose. The apothecary's assistant, a dark, handsome young man, waited on her, and looked with obvious appreciation upon his pretty young customer. That evening he brought the package around to the Knights' hotel and stayed to pay a call. "When he bade me farewell," Fanny wrote, "he handed me a small note and requested me to read and answer it. Its contents surprised me exceedingly . . ." The young Egyptian had written:

. . . Were I only charmed by your beauty, I would perhaps have won my passion, but love in its full extent has darted my heart. In declaring to you my intentions I do but follow its dictates. They are, to offer you my hand, for my heart has ever since been captivated by you. . . . I beg you to let me have an answer on the subject; howsoever it may be, let me be acquainted with it, for on your accepting or declining it depends my happiness for life, or total despair. . . .

But Fanny did not reply.

Fanny and her parents sailed up the Nile in a boat very much like
those above. The passing of two boatloads of friends on the Nile,
thousands of miles from home, was not considered unusual; in that
pre-income-tax era, a journey to Egypt was not rare. Up the river at
Thebes, for example, the Knights anchored beside the boat of Mr.
Knight's London banker. In Cairo, they saw a procession (below)
honoring the Feast of the Circumcision and celebrating a wedding.

# *"New York looks...
somewhat shabby"*

In the last week of July, John and Frances Knight and their daughter boarded the iron-hulled paddle steamer *Persia,* pride of the Cunard Line, bound for home. They reached New York on August 3 and Fanny, in one of her last travel-diary entries, wrote: "New York looks very lively and bustling and somewhat shabby, but how glad I am to be at home again! . . . I tell Pa that, after being so long in Europe, I will be entirely forgotten by all my friends, and in my old age will feel myself a stranger in my own land, should all my youth be spent in foreign countries. I am still proud of being a daughter of America, and will ever prefer my motherland to any other. . . . Pa has decided that we shall pass the winter in New Orleans, so I shall see HIM again!!"

"Him" was Thomas McDannold, a young New Orleans lawyer who had been attracted to Fanny during a previous meeting, who would remain her ardent suitor through four years of war—he served with a Louisiana regiment in nineteen major battles—and who would finally win her hand in 1867.

Throughout the remainder of her life Fanny never forgot her Grand Tour. For whatever might be said, then or now, about the snob appeal of such a sojourn, it *was* an education, one which would have been hard to match. In a few brief years—and those her most impressionable ones—young Fanny Knight had seen at firsthand many of the crowned heads of Europe. She had seen the fruits of one revolution—in France—and the seeds of another—in Czarist Russia. She had been introduced to the cultures of the ancient world, of the Renaissance, and of her own time. And she had visited most of the countries whose emigrants would, in the next half century, so profoundly alter the character of her own.

It was an expensive education, to be sure (the first two years alone, John Knight calculated, cost him over $12,000), but it was infinitely superior to the provincial female seminaries which were the only institutions of higher learning then available to women in the United States—even to the daughters of the wealthy. For a young woman with Fanny's spirit, curiosity, and quick mind, the Grand Tour was a treasure that sustained her richly to the end of her days.

---

*Alexandra Lee Levin, granddaughter of Fanny Knight, lives in Baltimore. She is now at work on a study of English women playwrights of the eighteenth century.*

## CUNARD LINE.
### Established 1840.
#### BETWEEN
### Liverpool, Boston, and New York
Calling at Cork Harbor.
From New York every Wednesday and Saturday.
From Boston every Saturday.
RATES OF PASSAGE
Cabin, $80  $100 and $130 according to accommodation.
Return tickets on favorable terms.
Steerage, at lowest rates.
For further information apply to.
C. G. FRANCKLYN, 4 Bowling Green. N. Y.

*The Knights came home on the Cunard Line, then building its supremacy over the transatlantic passenger traffic.*

*Fanny spent her first winter at home in New Orleans, where she received this invitation to a Mardi gras festival. Among the treasured souvenirs of their Grand Tour was John Knight's passport (right), stamped by the consular officials of half a dozen foreign nations.*

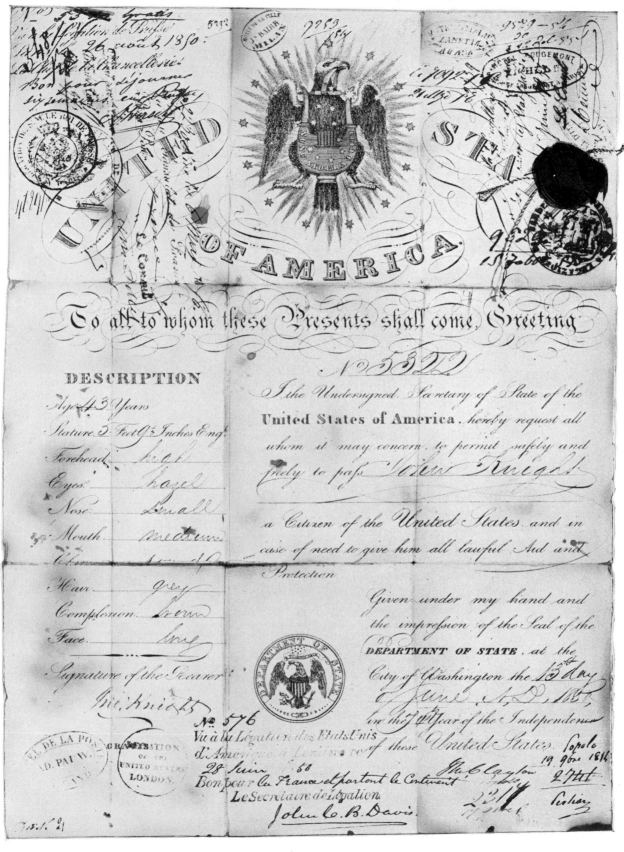

UNITED STATES OF AMERICA

To all to whom these Presents shall come, Greeting

N° 5322

I, the Undersigned, Secretary of State of the **United States of America**, hereby request all whom it may concern, to permit safely and freely to pass *John Knight* a Citizen of the *United States*, and in case of need to give him all lawful Aid and Protection.

Given under my hand and the impression of the Seal of the **DEPARTMENT OF STATE**, at the City of Washington the 13th Day of June A.D. 185_, in the 74th Year of the Independence of these United States.

**DESCRIPTION**

Age 43 Years
Stature 5 Feet 9½ Inches Eng.
Forehead high
Eyes hazel
Nose small
Mouth medium
Chin _____
Hair grey
Complexion brown
Face long

Signature of the Bearer

Jn°. Knight

N° 576

Vu à la Légation des États-Unis d'Amérique à Londres ce of these

28 Juin 1856
Bon pour en France et partout le Continent
Le Secrétaire de Légation

John C. B. Davis

Three Americans created the art of the motion picture, and

made it the universal language of the twentieth century

# The Moving Image

## By ROBERT GESSNER

The older arts, all seven of them—architecture, dance, drama, literature, music, painting, and sculpture—had their origins in the Mediterranean basin several thousands of years ago. The only new art, and the most universal, was born near the mouth of the Hudson River, and within the memory of living men. Three American geniuses—Thomas Alva Edison, Edwin Stanton Porter, and David Wark Griffith—individually and with others, created here a new means of depicting life.

This is the Moving Image, the eighth art, and today it is seen in living rooms, theaters, drive-ins, museums, classrooms. It is colored and black-and-white, wide and narrow, and often accompanied by voices, sounds, or music. It is free, subsidized, and charged for, preserved on celluloid and tape, transported in cans, over cables, through the air. It is projected on screens, shot from tubes, sometimes instantaneous, and always alive. It is the art of the twentieth century, and in the verbal confusion of our times it is also called cinema, film, motion picture, talkie, and television.

It is no archaeological accident that the oldest record of man's creative impulse (25,000 B.C. in the Pyrenees) is his effort to capture *motion*. The Cro-Magnon artist-huntsmen in their Lascaux cave paintings sought to hold life in motion by giving their wild bison the illusion of movement. The more modern art of literature, according to William Faulkner, "is really on its way back to the picture writing in the Neanderthal cave."

The first man to relate photography to the illusion of motion was an American, Coleman Sellers, a descendant of that notable family of artists and tinkers, the Peales. In 1860 Colonel Sellers, a mechanical engineer in Philadelphia, posed his sons in six photographs, showing them in the process of pounding a nail into a box—a parental impulse that has subsequently enriched the Eastman Kodak Company. Sellers mounted the photographs on the blades of a revolving paddle wheel, thus revealing his sons through a fixed peephole, in continuous, if jerky, motion.

Previously, a variety of Europeans—English, Belgian, Austrian—had experimented with hand-drawn applications of the theory that Peter Mark Roget (the *Thesaurus* man) had presented in a paper before the Royal Society in 1824. In a sense, no picture ever moves. All moving images are series of still pictures, flashed before the eyes at a speed faster than the eye can catch. This visual phenomenon (sixteen frames to the second for silent pictures, twenty-four for sound, thirty in television) permits a trick on the optic nerve, giving the illusion of constant motion. This trick Roget called "the persistence of vision."

The crucial question was how to photograph motion.

A wager of $25,000 by a California railway magnate and sportsman, Leland Stanford, started motion photography on its way. A battery of twenty-four cameras was set up at the Stanford stock farm in Palo Alto, to prove that a horse had all four feet off the ground at a given moment. The horse's hoofs were to trip a wire—an electrical device worked better—that clicked each camera. The photographer in charge, the eccentric but accomplished Eadweard Muybridge, later used the system to record the first strip tease, the first fat lady dance, the first muscle man exercising, all printed in a fascinating book, *Animal Locomotion.*

In February, 1886, Muybridge had the brilliant

# EDISON, or
# MOTION CAPTURED

The basic inventions necessary to bring photographs to life were made by Thomas A. Edison and his assistant W. K. L. Dickson—who also took the picture of the Wizard that appears below. Dissatisfied with their efforts to record motion on cylinders, as in the commercially successful phonograph, Edison and Dickson finally obtained from George Eastman of Rochester a fifty-foot strip of film which they perforated and made to move behind a lens, stopping just long enough for each frame to be photographed. Edison's Kinetoscope, in which the film was shown inside a peep-show box, was finally unveiled to public view on Broadway, in New York, on April 14, 1894, and caused an immediate sensation. In the next few years, Edison got many New York stage stars to perform before his camera in West Orange, New Jersey, among them Crissie Sheridan (right)—wife of Phil Sheridan of Flynn & Sheridan, an itinerant stock company—who did this "Butterfly" dance in 1897.

ALL PHOTOGRAPHS FROM THE LIBRARY OF CONGRESS

cal event, *The Execution of Mary Queen of Scots,* by William Heise, an Edison employee, was shot in August, 1895. More important, it also used the first trick shot. (The shot—a single camera operation covering an action, idea, or emotion—is the fundamental unit of this new language.) In the first shot of *The Execution* a young actress in a long black dress stands before the chopping block. She kneels, places her head on the block. The executioner raises the axe over his head, and swings. The shot ends. The second shot discloses the axe continuing its swing and chopping off the head of a sawdust dummy. End of shot. End of first classic.

By 1895, owners of penny arcades and exhibitions were demanding a machine similar to Henry Renno Heyl's version of the magic lantern, which had packed 1,600 customers into Philadelphia's Academy of Music a quarter of a century earlier. Edison was reluctant to return to the screen, in view of the popularity of his peep-show boxes. The steady flow of pennies from the arcades was convincing evidence for him. "The throwing of the pictures on a screen was the very first thing I did with the Kinetoscope," he told the New York *Sun,* April 22, 1895, on the occasion of a demonstration by Woodville Latham, who had infringed his patent. "I didn't think much of that, because the pictures were crude, and there seemed to me to be no commercial value in that feature of the machine."

However, the handwriting (and the screen) was on the wall. Others were experimenting with projection machines, and it was Thomas Armat of Washington who produced the mechanism that made possible the modern projector. Dickson had used the red-cross gear of the Swiss watchmakers to turn the sprockets and the film in intermittent motion, permitting each successive image an instant of rest and illumination. Armat chose the Maltese cross, whose flared ends would permit a steadier and clearer flow of image frames. He ordered a "mutilated" gear from the Boston Gear Works, in Boston, Massachusetts, and it worked beautifully, but with a roar. On the night of April 23, 1896, Armat's Vitascope, acquired by Edison, had its Broadway debut at Koster and Bial's Music Hall, approximately on the spot where R. H. Macy today sells lingerie. Thomas Alva Edison was an honored guest in a box; Armat was discreetly quiet in the noisy projection booth.

The distinguished theatrical magnate Charles Frohman was in the audience. "That settles scenery!" he cried to a reporter. "Painted trees that do not move, waves that get up a few feet and stay there, everything in scenery we simulate on our stages will have to go. Now that art can make us believe that we see actual, living nature, the dead things of the stage must go." The New York *Herald* reporter was eloquently matter-of-fact: "Mr. Edison calls his latest invention the Vitascope which he says means a machine showing life, and that is exactly what the new apparatus does."

Thus the Moving Image was born. What the inventors Edison, Dickson, and Armat did was nothing less than create a new and universal language, a way of recording people, places, and things *in motion.* To appreciate how this language developed into an art, it is essential to understand its unique characteristics, the three basic types of visual motion, as separate and interrelated as words, phrases, sentences.

For a start we might think of recorded movement as the nouns and pronouns of the new language. A face smiles, a wind moves the trees, a fire engine races up the street. In Edison's time, recorded movement was mainly vaudeville, news, staged scenes—as it still is today. Not until Edwin Stanton Porter, an employee of Edison, added his own contribution did the Moving Image reveal its full potential.

Porter added mounted movement, or editing, which might be thought of as the verbs of the visual language. He took the novelties of his European contemporaries—the close-up shot, the panoramic shot, the tracking shot, the multiple sets, the inserted and edited shots, the chase—and lifted them to the level of cinematic drama. Porter, more than anyone, translated the novelty of the Kinetoscope into the craft of the motion picture. He remains, unfortunately, its unsung genius; his first masterpiece is not even mentioned in the latest history of the art.

Edwin Stanton Porter was born in 1870 in the small Pennsylvania town of Connellsville on the Youghiogheny River. He had a quiet face, sad eyes, and sandy, drooping mustaches. One brother, Harry, became a gold miner in California; two other brothers and an unmarried sister settled in New York City. Edwin joined the Navy. On his discharge, he remembered two Connellsville men who had invested in the Vitascope with high hopes of making a fortune. It was a time when almost everybody seemed to be making, or talking about making, fortunes. Porter thought of trying his luck with the new horseless carriages. Instead, in New York that spring of 1896, he walked into 43 West Twenty-eighth Street, in the area around Broadway, which was fast becoming the world's motion-picture center. He called on Raff and Gammon, Edison's agents for the Vitascope, and was put to work operating projectors.

The humid air around Broadway that summer was hot with competition and patent infringement. At about the time he became aware that Raff and Gam-

CONTINUED ON PAGE 100

# GRIFFITH, or
# MOTION INTERPRETED

*To the task of making films, David Wark Griffith brought the temperament of an actor and a poet. He used the devices of lighting and camera manipulation to suggest emotions, set moods, and convey abstract ideas—thus enabling the movie language to be more subtle and expressive. In* Edgar Allan Poe (1909) *he accentuated light and shade by turning a klieg light through a window on the poet's unhappy garret (right). In Griffith's film, Poe is comforting his sick wife when a raven appears, inspiring him to write a poem, which he then attempts to sell to editors. Turned away by one, he finds another who will give him ten dollars, and returns to his wife's bedside only to find that she has expired. Griffith had a sentimental streak that responded to Poe, but eventually lost him his popularity with the public. He made and spent several fortunes, never took his own film work seriously, and thought that the movies would not last. "I give them a few years," he said.*

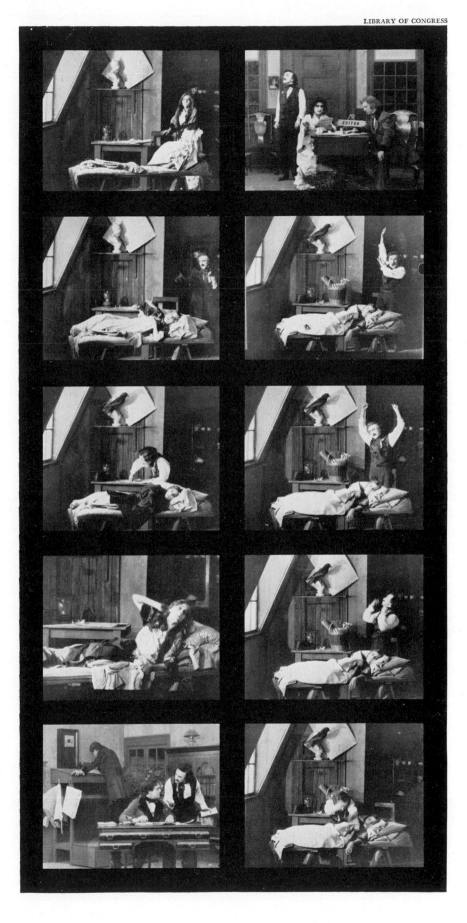

*By* PETER LYON

# The Fearless FROGMAN

It was thirty miles offshore, and stormy, but the daredevil swimmer plunged into the Atlantic with a crisp "Goodnight, ladies and gentlemen!" Our author recalls bold Captain Boyton, a mixture of Jules Verne, Tom Swift, and a bit of Walter Mitty.

**W**ell out to sea from New York and bound for Liverpool, Captain Bragg, master of the steamer *Queen,* was consternated one October evening in 1874 to see a figure clad in rubber from head to foot appear suddenly from under a lifeboat and waddle purposefully toward the rail. He raced from his bridge to lay hands on the apparition, which, as he could now see, was bristling with all the equipment of an Eagle Scout in parade uniform: canteen, food canister, axe, signal lights, rockets, compass, knife, and small double-bladed paddle.

"Where do you think you're going?" he demanded.

"Ashore," said the figure, and added remorsefully that this was his only course, for he was a wicked stowaway.

Since the nearest shore was 250 miles away, Bragg sensibly concluded he had collared a madman. He insisted on peeling off the rubber garment, to discover within a lean, merry, Dublin-born adventurer named Paul Boyton, apparently quite sane except for his determination to jump overboard in mid-ocean.

But Captain Bragg would have none of this. Instead he gave Boyton a place at the officers' mess and for the next week listened round-eyed to his guest's

*In full rubber regalia, Captain Boyton, opposite, posed for a Budapest photographer during his triumphant tour of European rivers. In his right hand is his brass signalling horn.*

casual reminiscences. At fifteen, it seemed, Boyton had joined the Union Navy; in the decade since the Civil War he had been a revolutionary in Mexico, a franc-tireur in the Franco-Prussian War, a participant in the short-lived Paris Commune, a conspirator in a plot to free Cuba from the Spanish yoke, a South African diamond miner, and the captain of the first lifesaving service at Atlantic City, in which capacity he had personally plucked seventy-one bathers from the claw of the sea puss. Gradually it dawned on Bragg that here was no ordinary harum-scarum daredevil, but a man with a positive genius for recklessness, who staked his life the more zestfully as the odds against him rose. He asked his guest about the rubber suit.

This was the invention of a Pittsburgh manufacturer, C. S. Merriman, designed as a lifesaving device for transatlantic steamship passengers. Supple and absolutely watertight, the suit had compartments for air behind the head, at the back, at the chest, and along each thigh; in it, with only his face exposed, a man could float vertically or go skimming along on his back, propelled feet first by a paddle at the rate of one hundred strokes a minute; the suit was, in effect, a kayak. Already Boyton had paddled for miles out to sea off the Jersey coast, but he was seeking a sterner test. For this he had stowed away, and as the *Queen* neared the Irish coast, Captain Bragg decided he should have his chance.

On the evening of October 21, some thirty miles off-

37

shore, the glass was ominously low and the *Queen* rolled in a sullen sea, but Boyton was unperturbed. Overside he went. They heard his cheerful call: "Goodnight, captain! Goodnight, ladies and gentlemen!" Then he was alone, in the turbulent night.

That was at nine o'clock. By eleven the sea was raging under a westerly gale, and before dawn fifty-six vessels would be smashed on the shores of the British Isles, but Paul Boyton paddled on. Thirty miles he paddled, past the Cape Clear light at the southernmost tip of County Cork, and then up Roaringwater Bay to Skibbereen. The barefoot fisherfolk refused to believe him, but by the time he got to Cork, the cables had carried his story, and two continents were acclaiming him as a hero. A hero, moreover, with a new and incredible dimension added, for here was a man apparently as much at home in the water as on land. Such a circumstance was the more extraordinary since, at the time, ocean swimming was still an exotic pastime; folk feared the salt water might "leach away the essential salts of the body"; where timidity was the rule, Boyton seemed the more audacious. One hundred thousand curious flocked to watch him paddle down the Liffey and across Dublin Bay from Howth Head to Dalkey; more scores of thousands came to see him float down the Thames; Queen Victoria received him at the Isle of Wight and presented him with a gold chronometer.

He was more than a hero: he was a prodigy; was there anything he could not do? The more venturesome began to propose for him unheard-of hazards: dared he attempt the English Channel? But of course. Boyton gobbled challenges as lesser mortals nibble bread. To the accompaniment of intense excitement, he essayed the Channel in May, 1875; he paddled tranquilly from Cape Gris-Nez to Fan Bay, enjoying his lunch and puffing on a cigar as he went; on arrival he was welcomed by an eleven-gun salute and a cablegram from President Grant.

The Rhine, the Rhone, the Seine, the Po, the Loire, the Tiber, the Tagus; the Strait of Gibraltar, the Bay of Naples, the Strait of Messina—and later the Mississippi, the Missouri, the Yellowstone, the Ohio, the Hudson. He negotiated them all, sometimes trailing a tiny boat he called the *Baby Mine,* in which he stowed food and cooking equipment for his meals en route. Cigars were named after him; hundreds of columns in newspapers lauded his watery exploits; his income from exhibitions soared to $2,000 a week; editorials gravely insisted his suit should be standard equipment on seagoing vessels.

After a time, however, merely floating downstream began to pall on Boyton: true, it was wet, but where was the risk? He had had a surfeit of safety. Then Peru got embroiled with Chile in one of their periodic struggles, and Boyton's spirits revived: here at last was an opportunity to get blown to smithereens. He entered the Peruvian naval service and, as he told it, paddled silently out, under cover of night, to a Chilean man-of-war, affixed to her 125 pounds of dynamite, and thereby broke the Chilean blockade—though Peru lost the war. When he returned to New York he held the rank of captain in the Peruvian Navy.

He returned to retire, since there seemed, regrettably, to be no other ways in which he could threaten his personal actuarial balance. To shake the water out of his ears and capitalize on his fame, he opened a bar and grill at 38 West Twenty-ninth Street in New York; he called it The Ship, and it became a favorite haunt of Manhattan sports. To relieve his tedium, he was reduced to playing pranks on Her Majesty's Royal Navy.

In May, 1885, the British lion was irritable. His tail was being tweaked by the Irish; there had been some incidents involving dynamite; one of the chief Fenian leaders, Jeremiah O'Donovan Rossa, was trumpeting his defiance from a Manhattan sanctuary. Additionally, the lion's tail was being yanked by Imperial Russia over a border dispute in northwest Afghanistan; contemporary statesmen fancied they could descry war clouds lowering. While this minuscule crisis was bubbling, a Russian corvette, the *Strelok,* and a British man-of-war, the *Garnet,* had coincidentally dropped anchor in New York Harbor, and Boyton therefore undertook to soothe the dolors of the moment by showing how simple it would be to blow the *Garnet* out of the water. If he was shot in the process, why, then the laugh would be on him; but he did not propose to get shot.

As privily as possible, considering that he was attended by two or three friends and a noisy gaggle of newspaper reporters, Boyton went to the docks with a dummy torpedo, found a boatman named Steve Connors, and told him he planned to attach it to the hull of the *Garnet.* "Oh, wurra!" said the boatman, according to the accounts, eyeing the cigar-shaped, four-foot dummy. "Oh, Rossa! a dirrty, desprit business!" His eyes glowed. "For five dollars I'm in for the night wid yez."

The conspirators were first rowed across the Upper Bay to Staten Island. They proceeded to the barroom of the Bay View Hotel to fortify their spirits against the night's sinister enterprise, and here they were nearly foiled before they had fairly begun. For the barroom was full of British bluejackets, and all hands eyed the group of newcomers curiously. What were they up to, in their dark slouch hats and with their coat collars turned up? To allay suspicion, one of the reporters remarked casually, in a clear, carrying baritone, "I'll bet a fiver the white dog licks the brindle." The others accepted his gambit, and for a few minutes there was lively talk of an imaginary fight to be staged between two imaginary bull terriers. The bluejackets went back to their beers.

But the talk had aroused one righteous citizen, and he slipped out to notify the police. Before long the place was surrounded by Staten Island constabulary intent on halting the illegal dogfight. Plaintively the reporters now insisted that their talk had all been a joke. A hack driver who had been nursing his drink in a corner, and who had confidently expected to earn a pretty penny by transporting all the sports to their fighting pit, was so disturbed to find his wages vanishing that he lost his temper and slugged a reporter. That did it. Everybody was arrested.

It took Boyton and his party an hour to talk themselves out of captivity, but fortunately, when they made their chastened way back to the Bay View Hotel, they found that the bluejackets had all returned to the *Garnet*. The atmosphere was serene. Boyton led the way down to the shore.

The *Garnet* lay in the Narrows off Staten Island, two lights at her masthead. Boyton, having clad himself in his rubber suit and lighted a cigar, slipped silently into the water, towing the torpedo behind him. He meant to paddle beyond the British ship and then float down upon her on the tide; but on his first cast he came, instead, alongside an American cutter. She seemed to be too small to be the *Garnet*, so he called out, "What vessel is this?" An astonished American marine answered that it was the *Endeavor*.

"Well, then, let me come alongside and take away a torpedo I've tied to her by mistake."

"For God's sake, take it away quick!"

Boyton paddled away for a second try. Across the water the voices of his party came to him; Connors was rowing them out near the *Garnet;* half the party had started to sing "God Save the Queen" whilst the other half had struck up "Is This Mr. Reilly?" Boyton heard Connors exclaim, "Byes, this is dirrty work," and a moment later, "Oh, Rossa, you're a daisy!"

By this time Boyton had lashed his torpedo to the *Garnet*, but his paddle made a chunking sound as he pulled to get away. At once came a voice, "Ahoy, there! What's that?"

"Only a log," answered Boyton, "floating in the water."

"Stop there! Who are you?"

"It's all right, gentlemen," shouted Boyton, paddling fast. "I'm only fishing! Trolling, you know! You've got a torpedo, fast to your vessel!" By this time he was out of pistol range, so he blew a blast on a trumpet he had slung round his neck, as a signal to his party to come fetch him. But behind him, aboard the *Garnet,* a bugle sounded the call to quarters, and before Boyton could be hauled aboard Connors' boat, here came a steam launch with a lieuten-

*At Lyons, France, he appeared in the medals that Europe showered on him. The people of the city presented the elegant poniard.*

ant, a midshipman, and a half-dozen bluejackets with their rifles cocked.

"Oh, wurra," moaned Connors. "Remember my poor suffering mother-in-law in the Twelfth Ward!"

Boyton's reaction to this armed party was characteristic. He clambered aboard the launch, grabbed a rifle leveled at his breast, and wrenched it from the bluejacket's hands, saying, "You can't shoot with that thing—I don't believe it's loaded." At once another

CONTINUED ON PAGE 92

The Wisconsin glacier, last of many, reached its limit 11,000 years ago. According to a theory recently proposed by Maurice Ewing and William Donn, each ice age came after a periodic melting of the Arctic Ocean by warm currents flowing through Bering Strait and over the Greenland-Norway sill. Open polar water provided moisture for the unending snows, layer upon layer, which then built up the massive ice sheet many thousands of feet thick.

*Footprints*

*The glacier that covered most of North America scarred the land,*

*turned rivers in their courses, and deeply influenced our history*

A narrow band of very low, very gentle hills extends across the northern states from Cape Cod to the Rocky Mountains in Montana. In places the winds and rains of thousands of years have worn them down to insignificant undulations; in other places they may be a hundred feet high or more. There is nothing about it to catch the casual eye, but the geologist recognizes this ridge as the terminal moraine of North America's last continental glacier, the line where the ice ended its long advance and began to melt back.

The glacier that stood on that line would have been a spectacular sight had there been anyone to see it: a great palisade of green and white ice many hundreds of feet high and stretching to the horizon east and west. For the most part, it probably loomed silently menacing, but from time to time huge sections crumbled off in awesome avalanches. Forests grew, and herds of woolly mammoths and other, less lordly creatures grazed almost up to the ice face, but to the north, atop the glacier, there was only a barren expanse of blizzard-swept ice stretching in absolute desolation toward the Arctic Circle.

The glacier was the last cataclysmic event that helped shape the face of the continent. North of the line of terminal hills, the land was drastically changed. Rock was rasped from mountains till the craggy buttresses were smoothed away and the valleys ground wider and deeper. Soil and gravel were stripped down to bedrock in some places, and the land level dropped as much as hundreds of feet deep in others. Myriads of lakes were gouged into the land, while rivers were dammed, diverted to new beds, and sometimes even shunted bodily from one drainage system to another. The effects of the ice sheet are not only still very apparent, they are often so marked as to have influenced the course of our history and helped to shape the economic pattern of the northern part of the continent. They have even had a strong effect in molding the character of some of our people.

If that last statement sounds extreme, consider that most individualistic type, the New England Yankee, and note well his relationship to his land. When the ice sheet ground its way across New England, it scoured off most of the soil down to the granite ribs of the land—and when it melted back much later, it dropped millions of boulders over the landscape to make the region even less promising. It is not exactly a fat and hospitable land, and the people who elected to live there have had to spend their lives contending with it for a living in a battle so close that they could not help but absorb some of the flintiness of their own fields.

If the New England rocks yielded a scant living, they were an excellent hone against which the wits of the men who lived among them were sharpened to a fine edge, until "Yankee ingenuity" came to denote the ultimate in the ability to improvise and to get much out of little. At the same time, the streams that foamed through the uneven, glaciated hills provided abundant water power to put that ingenuity to work. As a result New England was, for a long time, the industrial heart of the nation.

What was the nature of this phenomenon that sent unbelievable quantities of ice grinding out of the north until more than half of North America was

# of the Great Ice

*By* RALPH K. ANDRIST

41

buried a mile or two deep? Contrary to popular belief, the ice did not form around the North Pole and then flow southward. It formed in a number of centers—Canada, Greenland, Europe, Siberia—more or less simultaneously, and spread from each of those places. Nor was the glacial era a period of unusual cold; the essential for a glacier's formation is only that more snow shall fall during the winter than can melt in summer.

And times have come when the winter snow has

ANSEL ADAMS

*Glacial "polish" in Lyell Canyon, Yosemite National Park*

outlasted the summer sun, not just for a few seasons but for thousands of years, piling up inch by inch, foot by foot, and packing into ice under its own weight until it came to be probably two miles or more thick at the center and hundreds of miles across. It was a burden so massive that it pushed the rock foundations of the land down into the molten magma on which they float. In many places the land is still springing back as the displaced magma flows back in currents of unbelievable ponderousness. The land in the Hudson Bay region, where the ice first started to accumulate and disappeared last, still has a long way to rise; it is estimated that eventually the bottom of the bay will emerge as dry land—provided another glacier does not come first.

As the ice became thousands of feet deep, the enormous pressure began to force the great mass outward at the edges. Meanwhile, the unending snows kept falling and turning to ice, always maintaining the pressure and keeping the glacier pushing forward, grinding rocks to pebbles and pebbles to clay and sand, and moving incredible quantities of rock and earth over the face of the land.

The glacier eventually reached its limit when weakening forward movement was just balanced by the rate at which the ice front was melting back, a period

42

of equilibrium that probably lasted for hundreds of years, during which there were only minor fluctuations of the ice front. During this time, the glacier acted as a giant conveyer belt, carrying forward great quantities of boulders, gravel, and clay embedded in the ice, which were exposed and dropped at the melting front of the ice mass. In this way were amassed the great drifts, or moraines, that still trace the forward limit of the glacier.

The most easily identifiable stretch of moraine was laid down in the East, where the glacier stopped with its leading edge a number of miles offshore from the present coast. Much of the tremendous burden it dropped still abides, though considerably worn away by the sea; its largest portions are Long Island, Block Island, Martha's Vineyard, Nantucket, and Cape Cod. Here, for what comfort it may give some Vermonter or New Hampshireman fighting poverty on a hard-scrabble farm, is much of the earth that once clothed his hillsides.

To the west, the ice just buried Manhattan and stopped with an advanced lobe resting on Staten Island. Its line bent to the north in Pennsylvania because the mountains, while unable to stop it, did hold it back somewhat. It reached almost to the Ohio River in Indiana and Ohio, then tended in an irregular line northwestward until it came almost to the Canadian border in North Dakota, and then ran straight westward to the mountains. The western mountains were too high to be overrun, but they proliferated a rich crop of mountain glaciers that joined together into an almost solid icecap which connected with the continental glacier to the east.

There were other glaciers before the one we are concerned with, hundreds of thousands of years earlier. Some of them pushed farther to the south; dim remains of ancient terminal moraines show that ice has reached as far south as Louisville, St. Louis, and Topeka.

After pausing at its farthest-advance line, the glacier

ANSEL ADAMS

*A boulder field near Manzanar, Owens Valley, California*

*At its height, in the ranges of Alaska, the ice sheet might have looked approximately as the Chugach Mountains do today.*

began to melt back. It was hardly a precipitous retreat, because a mile-deep ice mass does not fade away in a summer or two. During the period in which it was melting back through New England, the Connecticut River valley was a lake and thus provided a sort of measured course over which we may time the rate of retreat. Each summer a thin layer of sandy sediment settled to the bottom; each winter an even thinner one of fine silt drifted down. Each pair of layers, called a varve, indicates the passage of a year just as plainly as does a ring on a tree. From a painstaking count of these varves, geologists find that it took more than four thousand years for the ice to melt from the present site of Hartford, Connecticut, to that of St. Johnsbury, Vermont, a sluggish average rate of only about one mile in twenty-two years.

But this, like all averages, is misleading because the retreat was not a steady one. Sometimes the ice melted back without interruption and dropped its load of debris in an even layer on the land. At other times the ice front would pause, balanced between its rate of melting and another time of forward movement, so that a ridge or "recession moraine" would be laid down. And occasionally a new forward surge would override and scatter earlier deposits.

So, both coming and going, the ice reshaped the land and left it far different from what it had been. Consider, for example, two of the many rivers it altered and rerouted. At one time the streams that now make up the headwaters of the Ohio flowed into Lake Erie; when the ice dammed the old courses, the water was forced to flow south and west around the glacier front until it found its way to a tributary of the Mississippi and so formed part of the Ohio River system. In the West, the upper Missouri also followed a different path; it flowed north into Canada until the ice blocked that outlet and made it find a new channel that also led to the Mississippi.

These two river diversions are especially interesting because of their subsequent effects on American history. The first settlers across the Allegheny Mountains found rivers that led toward the setting sun; and they underwent a quick change in economic orientation because all at once it was easier to ship their produce all the way to New Orleans by flatboat than to haul it by wagon a few dozen miles back across the mountains. The Missouri performed an equally important function. It was the only water route leading from the Mississippi into the western mountains at a point only a short distance across the continental divide from a river that flowed into the Pacific. It thus became the route of Lewis and Clark, and after them the surge of traders and mountain men who crossed to the Columbia River valley and so established the firm American claim to the Pacific Northwest.

The last continental glacier is only the latest of four which came and went during the Pleistocene epoch. Geologists sometimes refer to the era as the "last ice age" in recognition that there were other—and more severe—periods of glaciation back through the dim mists of time. The first of the four "recent" glaciations, called the Nebraskan, came an estimated one million years ago, and was

43

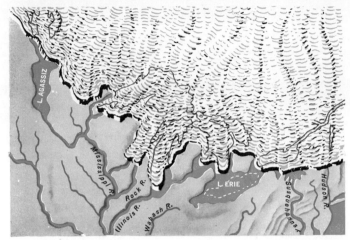

*When the glacier finally retreated, it left behind lakes and rivers in the shapes we know now. The Great Lakes, previously an area of broad lowlands, were formed in depressions gouged and deepened by lobes of the ice sheet as it expanded. When the ice withdrew,*

followed in turn by the Kansan, Illinoian, and finally, the Wisconsin glaciations. Geologists have named them from the areas where their traces were most clearly identified and studied; the glaciers that occurred at the same time in Europe have completely different appellations. Between the times of ice, there were long interglacial periods when the climate grew mild, and most of the work of the glaciers was erased by a hundred thousand or more years of erosion.

Although scientists have generally agreed on a chronology of the comings and goings of ice, they are the first to admit that the dates are only the best possible estimates. But about one event there is little guesswork; we know almost exactly when the last glacier reached its southern limit. It so happened that a final surge of the ice overran a spruce forest near what is now Two Creeks, Wisconsin, snapping off the big trees and burying them deep under sand and gravel. Nuclear physicists, by a method recently discovered, are able to determine quite accurately the age of a bit of organic matter by finding what degree of radioactivity still remains in the carbon it contains. Complex Geiger counter tests of Two Creeks spruce proved that the forest had died approximately eleven thousand years ago, give or take a century or two. It was a result that confounded many scientists who had placed the peak of the glaciation at least twenty-five thousand years ago, but subsequent radioactive carbon datings from many sources have since corroborated the readings from the Two Creeks wood.

Eleven thousand years is not a long time, geologically speaking. The ice-torn land has mellowed in that time, but the softening is only superficial and our northern landscape is still basically a glaciated one. Just as the ice left the altered Ohio and Missouri

rivers to show it had passed that way, it also produced many other monuments to its action.

The most spectacular of these is the Great Lakes. All four glaciers played a part in producing them, each one scooping the basins a bit deeper, until the last, the Wisconsin glacier, left their beds pretty much as they are today. The Great Lakes are the earth's largest body of fresh water and comprise its greatest inland waterway. From the days of the French explorers they have been an avenue into the heart of the land, one which has become even more important with the opening of the St. Lawrence Seaway. It is the further good fortune of America that the lakes are rimmed with rich deposits of iron and coal, which have been laced together with cheap transportation to form the greatest industrial complex in the world.

When it formed the Great Lakes, the glacier also increased their usefulness by providing good access to them to supplement the St. Lawrence outlet. As it melted back, the glacier not only filled the lake basins but also formed an enormous dam to prevent excess water from draining across the lowlands to the north. The overbrimming water had only one place to go; it burst through to the south in several mighty torrents.

One of these was the great river that tore a channel from Lake Erie to the Hudson River. The Mohawk River now flows in the eastern part of the valley, which has been a strategic pathway between Lake Erie and the Hudson ever since the French and English started squabbling over North America. Its most important period, however, began in 1825 with the opening of the Erie Canal, which was dug in the bottom of the old glacial watercourse and brought a rush

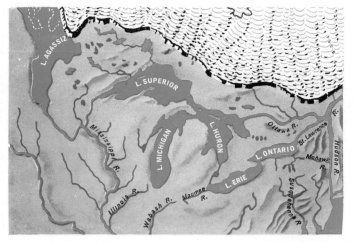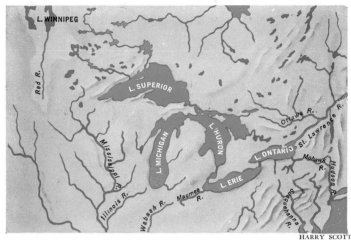

HARRY SCOTT

*water gathered in these hollows and spilled out through the Mississippi, Susquehanna, Mohawk, or the St. Lawrence—the only natural outlet remaining today. Lake Agassiz was five times larger than Lake Superior, but shallow, and eventually drained into Hudson Bay.*

of settlers into western New York and onward into the Northwest Territory.

Another overflow channel left Lake Erie at the point where Toledo now stands, and ran into the Ohio. The Maumee and Wabash rivers now follow the same valley, which became the route of the almost forgotten Wabash and Erie Canal, between Toledo and Evansville, Indiana, whose 452 miles made it the longest in the country. Although a financial failure, it had a big part in opening northern Ohio and Indiana to settlement and development.

Still another outlet ran across the site of Chicago and, via the present courses of the Des Plaines and Illinois rivers, to the Mississippi. Between 1836 and 1848 the Illinois and Michigan Canal was dug in this valley to tie Lake Michigan to the Illinois River, and thereby to the Mississippi. Another waterway, usually called the Drainage Canal, was constructed much later along part of the same route to do double duty as a carrier of both Chicago's sewage and water commerce to the Mississippi, but it did not supersede the old canal, which is still in use, a very rare survival of the heyday of canal building. (The Erie Canal, or its successor, the New York Barge Canal, cannot make the same claim because it was completely rebuilt and much of it relocated during this century.)

Although the Great Lakes are the largest glacier-created bodies of water, there are countless other lakes from the Dakotas to Maine and north into Canada. Minnesota alone has many more than enough to justify its tourist-attracting slogan of "Land of Ten Thousand Lakes," while in Canada they are so numerous and interconnected as to be virtually uncountable, since it is a matter of individual judgment where one ends and another begins.

These are the waters that bore the bark canoes of the Chippewas and Crees, and later of the *coureurs de bois*. The forests around them have provided many fortunes in fur and timber; a very respectable amount of pelts and lumber still come from among them, but today the lakes are producing an additional bonanza: recreation dollars. The lakes are all creatures of the ice sheet, some gouged out of the earth or even out of rock, others created by glacier-built dams, but most simply formed when ice water filled the hollows and valleys in the churned-up mass of glacial debris.

But the greatest of the glacial lakes is long since gone. Geologists call it Lake Agassiz, after the Swiss-American who pioneered in advancing, and securing acceptance for, the ice-age theory; at its greatest extent it filled the valley of the Red River of the North in Minnesota and North Dakota and covered most of Manitoba—an inland sea larger than all the present Great Lakes combined. It formed when the retreating glacier left the area clear, while still blocking the normal northward drainage of the Red River; the resulting lake grew larger as the ice melted back, until the time came when the glacier withdrew so far that the water could rush out into Hudson Bay.

The only remnants of Lake Agassiz are Lake Winnipeg and some swamps and smaller lakes, but its ancient bed is easy to identify—and valuable as farmland. When the lake lay over the land, the silt brought into it by wind and water slowly settled, adding only a fraction of an inch each year to its bed but continuing century after century until the lake bottom was covered dozens of feet deep and every irregularity was hidden. When the water went at last, it revealed a plain as flat as a floor and stretching to the horizon

CONTINUED ON PAGE 86

45

# Children
## *of the*
# Young Republic

*As the nation changed, so did its theories about raising youngsters. Prayed over or let run wild, and always the despair of foreign visitors, they have usually survived*

*By* GEORGE R. CLAY

A mid-nineteenth century English lady named Mrs. Mary Duncan complained that American parents not only encouraged their children to show off to guests, but if the little dears didn't happen to be home during your visit you'd have to go through the ridiculous business of looking at their portraits.

In a hitherto unexhibited trove of 160 American folk paintings collected by the late Mr. and Mrs. William F. Gunn of Newton, Massachusetts, and recently acquired by the New York State Historical Association, there were found to be no less than forty children's portraits of the sort that Mrs. Duncan must have been trapped into making polite British noises about. These are not sons and daughters of the rich, painted by fashionable artists trained in European traditions, but boys and girls of the village and town. They were portrayed, before the age of popular photography, by men who might have been apprenticed as sign painters, wall stencilers, or perhaps tinware decorators. Their "likenesses," for which one itinerant artist charged as little as $2.92 (including frame and glass), portray average young Americans of the early eighteen hundreds, dressed up in their Sunday best.

Looking at them today—at their docile, rather earnest expressions and stiff little bodies—it is difficult to imagine that, as Felix de Beaujour wrote in 1814, they "sparkle in the streets of American towns like field flowers in the springtime." Even Mrs. Duncan was impressed by the precociousness of American

children. "Little creatures feed themselves very neatly," she reported, "and are trusted with cups of glass and china, which they grasp firmly, carry about the room carefully, and deposit, unbroken at an age when, in our country mamma or nurse would be rushing after them to save the vessels from destruction."

Other foreign observers took a less kindly view of what they called "the assumption, self-assertion, and conceit" of children in the United States. "As soon as he can sit at table [the American child] chooses his own food, and as soon as he can speak argues with his parents on the propriety or impropriety of their directions," sniffed one Englishwoman. J. V. Hecke, a German visitor during the 1820's, frequently saw girls "in convulsive anger at their parents," and boys "in quarrel with old people pick up stones, and threaten to fling them at the head of the old man that wanted

## Sons and Daughters of New England

*The portraits on these pages are from the collection of the late Mr. and Mrs. William F. Gunn, now on exhibit at the New York State Historical Association in Cooperstown. The names of some of the painters have been preserved but those of the children, regrettably, are lost. The healthy young man at right, with his dog and leather-bound book, was probably persuaded to pose between 1815 and 1820, a period when his Napoleonic haircut was highly thought of.*

Republic were being encouraged to go out and meet life, to get ahead, to be precocious.

Lydia Huntley's upbringing comes close to the average: restrained, yet full of such innocent pleasures as dancing class; choir singing; reading aloud from "instructive books"; walks after tea in summer, or "a short sail on the quiet Yantic"; evening visits in the fall, when checkers and draughts, "apples and nuts . . . were the accustomed and adequate entertainment"; in winter, late-afternoon sleigh rides out to some reputable country tavern, where a group of boys and girls ("composed of the sons and daughters of neighbors") would dance a few quadrilles and "cotillons," then return.

After one of these sleighing parties, Lydia's girl friend dashed off a note to her which is redolent with the sentimentality and hearty innocence of the age:

Dearest L:

Did not we have a good time last evening? Such a moon! We might have seen to work muslin by it . . . I declare it was romantic. The horses enjoyed themselves too. I know they did by their prancing and seeming to keep time to the bells. I suppose they thought we got up that music for their especial merriment and behoof . . . We succeeded quite well with our new cotillon, did not we? . . . Brother thinks it would be a pleasant variety to sing a song or two just before leaving. What do you say? Would not it look too frolicsome? . . . Mother thinks he improves mightily, and grows more of a gentleman in the house since he has gone with us nice ladies to these sleighing parties. So she promises we shall go again. That's just right. To please her, and be so happy, and grow wiser too, all at the same time, is a very grand business. So good-bye for the present. Be a good girl, and mind every word your mother says.

B. Nevins

In 1856, almost exactly fifty years after the frolic described by "B. Nevins," Caroline and Anna Richards were invited on a similar sleigh ride. Caroline was thirteen, but Anna was only ten and their grandparents, with whom they lived in the village of Canandaigua, New York, told them they could not go. They asked if they could spend the evening with a school friend instead. Their grandfather said yes, ". . . so we went down there and when the load stopped for her, we went too." The next day, Grandfather found out about it:

We knew how it was when we got home from school, because they acted so sober, and, after a while, Grandmother talked with us about it. We told her we were sorry and we did not have a bit [of a] good time and would never do it again. When she prayed with us the next morning, as she always does before we go to school, she said, "Prepare us, Lord, for what thou art preparing for us," and it seemed as though she was discouraged, but she said she forgave us.

Caroline, and especially Anna, were constantly being mischievous ("Anna tied her shoe strings in hard knots so she could sit up later"), and more often than not their grandmother knew exactly what was going on. Once someone asked Anna whether the old lady still retained all her faculties; "Yes, indeed," she said, "to an alarming degree." When Grandmother heard that Anna had played hookey and told her she hoped she would never let anyone bring such a report again, "Anna said she would not, if she could possibly help it!" While Mr. Adams, a Boston relative and the head of Adams' Express Company, was visiting, Anna asked what Eve was made for; when no one could answer, she told them all: "For Adams' express company."

Overheard by a critical visitor from abroad, these remarks on the part of a young child might have sounded like downright insolence. Yet her grandparents not only tolerated it in Anna, they rather liked it. "He has the queerest voice and stops off between his words," Caroline wrote of the minister they had all just heard one Sunday. "When we got home Anna [nine at the time] said she would show us how he preached and she described what he had said about a sailor in time of war. She said, 'A ball came—and struck him there—another ball came—and struck him there—he raised his faithful sword—and went on—to victory or death.' "

"I expected Grandfather would reprove her," Caroline adds, "but he just smiled a queer sort of smile and Grandmother put her handkerchief up to her face, as she always does when she is amused about anything."

What emerges from Caroline's diary and others of this later period is a new sense of informality between parents and children, and at the same time a growing separation of their two worlds. Anna adores and makes fun of both her grandparents; Caroline calls Grandmother her "dear little lady" and thinks "she is a perfect angel even if she does seem rather strict sometimes." But the real center of Caroline's and Anna's life is in school, in Sunday school, in the myriad activities outside their home.

Home was where you lived, but you didn't learn about *life* there. The world was moving so fast that, while the older generation still could and did teach values to the young, it had less and less to pass on of a practical nature. Henry Wright learned all he needed to know right on his father's farm. At six, Lydia Huntley was helping her grandmother to make her father's shirts; she was encouraged, "when in the parlor with older people . . . to imitate their employments." Caroline and Anna did a certain amount of light work about the house—threading needles before going to school or straightening their things,

*Aged perhaps three and four, these two boys look out on the world with eyes full of early wisdom—and a hint of impudence?*

getting their room ready to be cleaned—but it was the merest token.

Since they were allowed their own pursuits, were judged more and more by standards adjusted to suit their age group, and were unexposed either to the neglect or to the arbitrary parental wrath of an earlier day, it is hardly surprising that the Richards girls and other mid-nineteenth-century children occasionally considered grownups rather superfluous:

Anna and I were chattering like two magpies today [reads Caroline's entry for Christmas, 1857] and a man came in to talk to Grandfather on business. He told us in an undertone that children should be seen and not heard. After he had gone I saw Anna watching him a long time till he was only a speck in the distance and I asked her what she was doing. She said she was doing it because it was a sign if you watched persons out of sight you would never see them again.

This facetious attitude toward adults would have puzzled Henry Wright, whose father ". . . allowed but little familiarity . . . a look, or a tap of his foot on the floor, was enough to guide us and keep us quiet." Probably both he and Lydia would have been amazed, and delighted, by Anna's Sunday satires. "One thing can never be effaced from my memory," Wright says, "the burden of the Sabbath." Lydia was overcome by "a sensation of weariness" as she replied to her father's Sunday grilling on the catechism.

It would be false to imply that, by 1850, the old fundamental principles of Christianity no longer formed the basis for the American child's religious life, or that the Christian duty of employing time to best advantage wasn't still one of the first lessons taught the young. It would be still more wrong to assume that fathers had lost their whip hand. What "Paw" said still went, even if he didn't say as much and said it differently. The concentration of authority that made the family such a strong unit lasted, fundamentally unchanged, at least until the middle of the century.

Yet well before that, profound underlying conditions had begun to weaken the patriarchal family: the rapid development of machine industry, which weakened family life by long factory hours and gave women and children financial independence; the westward migration that swelled to enormous proportions in the 1830's and 1840's, scattering relatives, dispersing households, and developing in its wake an intense

---

*George R. Clay, the author of this article on nineteenth-century children, is a free-lance writer who has published short stories in a number of magazines, principally the* New Yorker. *"I'm currently on the staff of the New York State Historical Association," he writes, "live in Cooperstown, and have five twentieth-century children."*

## Subjects Forgotten, Painters Remembered

**Upper left:** *Dress and ringlets notwithstanding, the whip and knife mark this youngster as a boy. He was set to canvas in 1848 by William Matthew Prior (1806–73), who was born in Maine, lived for a time in Portland, and died near Boston. The boy's coral necklace was then considered to be a preventive for one or another of the childhood diseases.*

**Lower left:** *Close examination shows that John Brewster of Connecticut originally portrayed this child with the left shoe on. Brewster, who left many impressive works, was born a deaf-mute, in 1766, but this painting speaks for his thoughts: "All right then, hold it if you insist!"*

**Upper right:** *The girl with the red doll and short hair— not so modern a fashion as we think—is believed to have been painted by Erastus Salisbury Field (1805–1900), the largely self-taught primitive whose subjects were often Biblical or classical allegories, or imaginary—like his enormous* Historical Monument of the American Republic.

**Lower right:** *The* Young Hammerer *bears on its back the brief and somber inscription: "Died Feb. 19th, 1844, Aged, 1 yr. 8 mo. 2 da." The artist, Joseph Whiting Stock of Springfield, Massachusetts, left a diary for the years 1842– 45, which records over nine hundred of his portraits.*

spirit of personal and political freedom; the gradual but steady urbanization and almost imperceptible secularization, which forced more and more once-familial responsibilities onto society and its institutions.

The most obvious symptoms of these complex social innovations were reported with blunt glee by foreigners like the Englishman John W. Oldmixon, who had come to kibitz on the sprawling young democracy: "Baby citizens are allowed to run wild as the Snake Indians and do whatever they please," wrote Oldmixon. The Comte de St. Victor observed that a child of the lower classes quits his parents "almost like the animal does." American children, Adam Gurowski noted, "make freely the choice of their intimacies, then of their church, of their politics, their husbands and wives."

No doubt these European observers gave a more or less accurate picture of what they saw, but few seemed to realize the essential difference between nineteenth-century Europe and America: that children had to learn, not to know their place in the New World, but how to make it.

"Why need a child's will be broken?" argued one perceptive American early in the century. "He will have use for it all."

He did a hundred and fifty years ago.

He still does.

# THE COAL KINGS COME TO JUDGMENT

When the anthracite miners downed tools in 1902,

economic feudalism went on trial

*By* ROBERT L. REYNOLDS

The highways leading south and west out of Scranton, Pennsylvania, wind through the graveyard of a dying industry. Its monuments are decaying company houses, boarded-up collieries, and mountainous piles of culm—the black, gravelly residue from the mining of anthracite coal.

Most of the area's younger men have moved away now, unwilling to endure the bone-wearying labor and irregular pay checks their fathers knew, or unable to get jobs at all in the dwindling number of underground shafts still open or in the strip-mining operations that gouge great scars across the face of the land. The obituary pages of the local newspapers tell the story plainly: when old miners die, their funerals bring their surviving sons and daughters—and there are many of them, for this was a prolific immigrant stock—from New York, New Jersey, and other nearby states where they have gone in search of a better life.

Anthracite is finished now, replaced by oil and gas. Yet only fifty years ago northeastern Pennsylvania was a prosperous region. For here, in a 500-square-mile triangle of low mountains, deep valleys, and sharp outcroppings of rock, lies nearly all of the country's hard coal, and at the turn of the century anthracite heated most of the homes, factories, and offices of the Atlantic seaboard. Along with food and shelter, it was a major necessity of life, and when in 1902 the supply was cut off by a bitter, five-month strike, the entire East was thrown into turmoil. The governor of Pennsylvania sent the state's entire National Guard into the coal fields to keep order. In Wall Street J. P. Morgan, who seldom worried, was very worried indeed. So, as winter neared, was New York's reform

mayor, Seth Low, who feared bloody coal riots in the streets. Before it was over, the strike had helped spark a national revolution in the relationships among employers, employees, and the federal government. It had also thrust into national prominence a young union leader named John Mitchell, launching him on one of the most brilliant yet heartbreaking careers in the history of American labor.

In Scranton and Wilkes-Barre, in Shamokin, Mount Carmel, and Shenandoah, there are still men and women who remember John Mitchell. An elderly Hazleton librarian, then a little girl, recalls being taken by her father to Mitchell's headquarters in a local hotel so that the child could shake the hand of a man who was making history. And many an immigrant miner's son remembers when the family parlor proudly displayed two pictures side by side: a chromo-

*For Union President John Mitchell (right) and for the country at large, the "breaker boys" (opposite) became a symbol of the anthracite strike of 1902. Their childish faces begrimed by the dust of the cold, dank breaker, they worked from dawn to dark for as little as 35 cents.*

*James M. Alden, a government survey artist, painted this view of San Juan Island's harbor (above) in 1860, during the boundary crisis with England. The disputed area—wild, remote, and economically worthless—is shaded in red on the map below.*

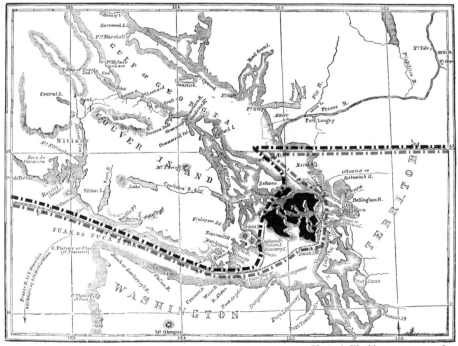

*Harper's Weekly*, OCTOBER 29, 1859

# One-shot War
## *with*
# England

*It lasted for years and the outcome was decided by the Kaiser.*

*The total casualties: one dead pig*

Perhaps the best, if silliest, war this country ever fought was caused by the death of a rooting pig. Though tediously long—it persisted, with extended periods of inactivity, for nearly thirteen years—it had one outstanding virtue: the pig was its only casualty. In addition, when this war (if so it can be called) was finally terminated, the nonbelligerent belligerents settled down to a century of remarkable peace and harmony.

It is difficult to exaggerate the tensions that time and again brought British-American relations to the boiling point in the half century following the War of 1812, or the skill and patience of responsible officials who managed to control the militant popular sentiment on both sides of the Canadian border. The bitterness resulting from a largely unresolved conflict was aggravated by the expansionist tendencies of the United States. Few politicians could withstand the temptation to draw cheers with the promise of annexing everything "from Tierra del Fuego to the Aurora Borealis." Meanwhile, the annexationists in the United States were successively abetted by malcontents among the Scotch-Canadians, the French-Canadians, and the British-Canadians, who used the issue to further their own political intrigues. Canada could hardly be blamed for feeling it might be swallowed up at any moment by its American neighbor.

The so-called Pig War began, as hostilities often do, over an affair of total insignificance. One day in the spring of 1859, a farmer killed a trespassing black pig with his musket. From this single rifle shot came volumes of diplomatic correspondence, countless threats, and nearly twenty years of anxious marching-up-the-hill-and-down-again.

The battlefield of this bloodless conflict was San Juan, one of a group of ruggedly attractive but economically worthless islands located at the southern end of the Strait of Georgia, between Vancouver Island and the Territory of Washington.

Behind the controversy was a long period of commercial rivalry between the British Hudson's Bay Company and American pioneers and fur traders in the Pacific Northwest. No violence mars the record, but would-be rivals to the company's monopoly in the area were quickly driven out by the basic tactics of outbidding, underselling, and pressure on the Indians not to do business with the intruders. At the same time, the antagonism of the Hudson's Bay Company had its limits. When American settlers caught by the Oregon fever of the 1840's straggled into Fort Vancouver at the mouth of the Columbia River, starving and destitute after their long trek across the continent, they were not turned away. Company officials tried to prevent them from settling north of the river but did not refuse the desperate travelers food and shelter while they recovered from their ordeal. The English seemed motivated less by the spirit of mercy than by the realization that cold-

*By* WARREN G. MAGNUSON

*Bushnell and his hired hands left Cincinnati, Ohio, by steamboat on April 5, 1866. In addition to Perry Case, Bushnell had employed two four-year veterans of the Union Army, Fred Lewis and Sid Bartlett, and Dick Bear, a bank clerk who made the trip for his health. This party of would-be cowboys arrived in New Orleans on April 13; and here Perry Case's story begins:*

At New Orleans we saw our first Texas cattle. They was loaded on cars to go east. And oh, such horses, Gawd! I never see such splendid horses!

Bushnell, talking with a man, says, "I am going to Texas after a load of cattle."

The man says, "You are aware that you can't buy Texas cattle with greenbacks, hain't you?"

"No," says he, "I don't know anything about that."

"Well," he said, "you can't buy a beef steer with a bushel basket full of greenbacks. Many can't read or write and can't tell a one from a twenty. They won't take paper. You will have to have gold."

We had two days to wait for the steamship. In the meantime Bushnell says to Dick and me, "Boys, we will go down to the bank here and get our money changed. You will have to go with me because it will be too heavy for one man to carry. We will divide it up. Each one will carry a third. It will be heavy enough then."

The cashier brought out the money in rolls of gold. My Gawd, we could never have carried silver. We went aboard the ship for the night. We always managed, on account of this money, to all be together as much as we could. Dick hid his money in his belt. I put mine in a handkerchief tied around my neck under my shirt.

Our ship, the *I. S. Harris*, left New Orleans next morning for Galveston, Texas. The Mississippi don't mix with salt water for two or three miles; you can see the muddy waters of the Mississippi far out in the bay. About that time it began getting rough. It wasn't what the sailors called rough, but it was rough enough that Bartlett, Bushnell, and Fred Lewis wasn't out of their berths the rest of the trip—two days and two nights. Dick would go to Fred twenty times a day and ask him if he was better just to hear old Fred stutter and spit, "O-n-no, b-b-b-by God!" Oh, he stuttered worse than any man I ever knew. And Dick would just die laughing.

When we landed in Galveston, we learned we had to wait until evening for a boat to Houston. At Houston we took a little railroad called Texas Central north to a little town called Millican. No grading was done, just ties laid down on the surface. The train ran slowly. Once the train stopped. We didn't understand and looked out, and there was the engineer off buying a pail of berries of some women picking beside of the tracks. We stopped for the

passengers to drink at a spring, and we stopped at every ranch.

At Millican we stayed at a hotel. After supper we was sitting on the veranda in front of the hotel smoking cigars. (They all call porches verandas there.)

We heard a revolver shot! A man cried out three times, each cry getting weaker. Dick jumped up and said, "That was a man shot."

I glanced around and saw everyone sitting still, not even taking their cigars out of their mouths. I pulled Dick by the pants to sit down. He was white as a sheet. The man's cries was terrible but I see every one sitting still.

Some boys came along going the way of the shots. It wasn't but a minute or two until back they come, and as they passed, one of the men took his cigar out of his mouth and said, "Who was shot, boys?"

"Oh, Texas Jack shot such and such a one."

The man said, "Kill him?"

"Yep."

Dick said, "Why did he kill him?"

"Oh," said the man, "probably just a tenderfoot."

"That Jack is a bad one," the other man said.

We gathered more about the fellow. They said he was quick on the draw and a sure shot. He knew everyone was afraid of him. He did not have to pay for what he wanted, horse or drinks. He took what he wanted and was likely to shoot the man for giving it to him,

cuits, the first I ha...
the ranch almost tw...
That was a treat. I ...
lage on the prairie...
Bob for the night...
asleep long when I...
lay still. I could not t...
well so I stayed th...
might be a plan to g...
my horse. Merryman...
lay. I said, "What is...

He said, "A nigge...
down here."

I didn't think it c...
lay still. That was ...
Bushnell. He could n...
go that bothered the ...
had told me some mo...
ble of Bushnell an...
drover at the time o...
crossing. It was worse...
posed. Bushnell said...
things when he got m...
ern drover because he...
out his cattle and le...
the only white man i...
a nigger. They woul...
That wouldn't go in...
know. They had bee...
hard years of war and ...

We started early ne...
the cattle. I was ...
dle of the stream whe...
me a sign. I always w...
pin right here on ...
everyone could see it.

---

Near Greenville the prairie was burning. It was one of the most beautiful sights I'd seen. Because of the pasture being destroyed we had to turn out of our way five miles. The cattle got scared of the fire and we had to be in the saddle all night, but it was a beautiful sight. Beyond Greenville, we camped with a preacher for the night. We had a good pen for the cattle, and the boys had all the ripe plums and blackberries they could eat. That was a treat!

One evening we camped early and lay resting around the wagon. Old Fred was cooking mess, while the first pickets of the night watched the cattle off a half mile or so. Gray Eagle suddenly threw himself on the ground and listened.

He said, "Indians—coming—fast—three."

We were just around the bend in a river at a sharp turn. We all heard horses coming then and jumped up with our guns loaded, ready. When they come around the curve, we yelled, "Halt!" We saw then to our surprise that one of them had a little white girl ahead of him.

I said, "Where did you get that child?"

One said, "Father kill brother."

I said, "And you stole her for revenge?"

The same one said, "Father kill brother."

I said, "Why did you kill your brother? Did your brother drive off his cattle and horses?"

They didn't say anything.

I said, "I don't want to take sides with you or the cowhands neither one, but this little girl must go back to her

---

mother and you g...
father comes back ...
They grunted an...
gave the little girl ...
took her back to ...
woman could not tal...
a time. She said she...
up clothes and the l...
house before she sa...
she had a gun and co...
was gone too far bef...
We was well up ...
and across the Red ...
tion.* One day I w...
of the herd when I ...
ing toward me. As I ...
he was staggering a...
he was about to fal...
an accident if a ma...
without a horse. W...
saw his face was c...
and his skull cut ...
clothes was soaked ...
I said, "Did the ...
He looked right ...
minute or more, th...
was that dazed.
I said, "Was yo...
ahead of us about a...
a long time he sai...
I took him up o...

* What is now the st...
in 1866, Indian Terr...
tions" among tribes ...
out of other parts of t...

---

or innocent men for no reason at all.*

The next day Bushnell was getting worse. The seasickness was getting the best of him. He did not get better of it. The doctor said, "You will have to lie still."

Bushnell was not better on the third day. In the evening we was sitting in the hotel lobby. I was playing a fiddle that was there. I looked up and saw Bushnell trying to come downstairs. He was hanging on the banister and could hardly make the steps. Dick jumped up to help him down. I says to the landlord, "Can't you give us a room downstairs? He is too weak to climb the stairs."

The landlord said there was only his room and the hired girl's room downstairs. The girl spoke up and said she would be glad to give up her room to help a sick man. So Dick went up for the medicine and our guns, and we took the girl's room for the night.

The next morning the landlord rapped at our door. Says he, "Is your room all right?"

We three, Bushnell, Dick, and me, always slept together when possible, with our heads against the door on account of the money.

The landlord couldn't get in.

I says, "Not up yet," and looked around. "Yes, we are all right."

"Then you are the only ones," says he. "Everyone in the hotel has been chloroformed and robbed. One of the girls, the one that changed rooms with you, has not come to, yet."

Fred and Bartlett had been robbed with the rest. Sid Bartlett lost thirty dollars. Fred Lewis would never tell how much.

During the three days in Millican we had picked up five ponies and was ready to start toward the cow country as soon as Bushnell was able to ride. When he said he would get out where they could not chloroform us, we packed up and started. We rode not more than a mile when we had to stop

* Though desperadoes were common on the Texas frontier, and murder was an all-too-frequent occurrence, one cannot help but feel that this "shooting" was a well-contrived hoax perpetrated on the credulous and still gullible northern "tenderfeet." [Ed.]

---

for him to rest. That was the way we traveled all day.

We rode slowly, resting often for Bushnell. It was just the end of the rainy season. No rain, but mud in the road to the axles. Oxen lay dead along the road where they had played out from pulling heavy loads in the deep mud. Carts stood stuck in the mud where the drivers had gone off and left them. We got twenty or twenty-five miles by the middle of the afternoon when we came to a plantation house. We liked to put up early because we didn't want to travel after dark, and we asked to stay all night at the plantation. The man asked us to "sit awhile" and a nigger took our horses.

It was an old plantation home just as it had been before the war. The planter's name was A. J. Moore. He treated us to everything that was the best. We had the first milk and butter that we had had since we arrived in Texas. In the evening when the Negroes came up from the fields there was forty mules and every one had a nigger wench riding. They were singing! Such a concert I never heard.

In the morning after breakfast they brought our horses. When we were ready to take leave, Bushnell asked what was our bill? I will never forget how that planter looked. He stared for a long time, then said, "I have never been guilty of taking money from a guest and I won't start on you."

You see, Bushnell did not understand these southern people. They were so hospitable. This man had fought four years in the Southern Army, but he treated us just as though we was from the South.

We hadn't got that day, oh, maybe three or four miles, when we come across a party of men with a dead man tied on a horse. We said, "What is the matter?"

They said they found him up above a little piece, tied to an Osage orange tree with sixteen bullet holes in him. He was a rider from the store at Millican and had took some merchandise from the store to the little store up above. Someone thought he had some money. He never carried any, but someone had thought so and shot him with sixteen bullet holes.

---

It was there we had a talk. I said, "You see the conditions and the country we are in, men shot down in cold blood, sharpers, robbers, bad men. Do you want to turn back, or go on? What do you want to do? We have this money and they know it. There has been an attempt to get it and we don't know what may happen."

"No," Bushnell said. Bushnell was no coward. "I don't want to go back home, but if I had known the conditions the country is in I never would have come."

"Well," I said, "you are an old man, sick, and need your rest. But here we are, four of us, Bartlett and Fred, two old soldiers, and Dick and me. One of us will always keep watch. They know we have this money." After that one of us watched every night.

*The progress of Perry Case and his companions into the Texas cow country was slow, for Bushnell was still ailing. On April 25, they reached the town of Waco on the Brazos River; another day's journey across the plains brought them to a ranch owned by a man named McCabe, from whom Bushnell purchased seven hundred head of cattle. McCabe also agreed to furnish experienced cowhands for the first part of the drive north, and to teach Bushnell and his men some of the rudiments of handling the tough, semiwild longhorns. Much of that instruction, however, consisted of riding the "greenhorn Yanks" through the thorny chaparral, or trying to get them lost. Even so, Perry Case had a fine time; his single regret was that one of McCabe's sons refused to sell him a beautiful sorrel colt named Bob. During the two-week interlude at the ranch, Perry had several opportunities to make side trips. On one of these sight-seeing jaunts with his friend Dick Bear, he confronted the desperado, Texas Jack. It was a meeting that nearly cost Perry Case his life, and when it was over he was glad that he had taken time during his stay at the ranch to practice with his six-shooter.*

Old McCabe said, "You want to get used to the saddle, how would you like to ride to Boiling Springs?" He told us about it. I asked how far it was.

night Dick and I lay down on cradle rolls with water all around us. The next day it rained. We slept on dung hills to get out of the water. There was nothing dry to burn and no fire to cook with. What we had to eat for a week was honey and crackers. The water we drank came from a mudhole. The boys all got the blues.

Then one night, came what the Texas boys called a "norther." The wind blew in from the north on our wet clothes and we almost froze to death. We put on our overcoats and could not keep warm then. Dick said he did not know it could be cold in hell. For two days and three nights we tried to get warm. Dick lay there one night; it was too cold to sleep. He said, "Perry, are you awake? Put your hand out." There under his arm was a little kitten, all curled up asleep. We did not know where she came from; there had been no house in ten miles. Dick put her in the wagon in the morning with Fred, and he let her ride.

After the "norther" the weather warmed up and it began raining again. One of them rainy nights we had an awful stampede. I was asleep on the ground and I heard the revolvers signal they was off. I called to Bob, but Bob was right there. He came running up and stopped. He stopped barely long enough for me to get my foot in the stirrup and he was off. We didn't have any time to lose. The steers came on fast, about on us. I wasn't afraid they could overtake us—they couldn't catch Bob if he could see—but it was so dark I couldn't see my horse's head before me. I wasn't afraid Bob would stumble. He never stumbled in his life, but I thought of them holes in the prairie, made by little prairie animals, where a horse running in the dark and not being able to see, might step and fall. Bob knew! He knew just as well as I did that he was running for his life as well as mine. All of a sudden I felt Bob halt—halt for just a fraction of a second and gather himself for a jump. I knew it was a jump and a big one; I was ready in the stirrup. He sprang into the air and it seemed we was off the ground two minutes. I wondered what it was and if there was any ground at all. I thought it must

be a wide gulch. . . . caught the groun . . . feet miss and go . . . the stirrup caugh . . . off the saddle, p . . . ing Bob with all . . . fought! He made . . . an instant for m . . . the stirrup, and . . . cattle went into . . . others over them . . . their breath. Af . . . cattle scattered a . . .

The next mo . . . back to gather up . . . in what they ca . . . head of cattle t . . . their necks, or c . . . way of the on . . . never saw it. Di . . . back he sat dow . . . I said, "What's . . .

He said, "Per . . . you jump that . . . must have jump . . . There is not a . . . have got over . . .

I knew it. T . . . in the herd th . . . it; not a horse a . . . especially.

We waited n . . . went ahead sco . . . one afternoon . . . Trinity was d . . . We had a cle . . . killed a beef a . . . a week. A little . . . herd. He was . . . kitten. I don't . . . from—there wa . . . for miles.

The next da . . . in the worst . . . know why Bu . . . place. We had . . . to drive throu . . . river went stra . . . a fast current. . . . mile drive to . . . It was late, a . . .

Somebody s . . . there was that . . . river like a d . . . complaint ab . . . day. Everybo . . . got up the b . . . the herd trai . . . was with ther . . .

I said, "What' . . . don't get these c . . . getting late. See . . . Why don't you . . .

Then says Bush . . . fellows won't let . . . tle; they say if . . . go across."

"The hell they . . . know the roughes . . . to laugh yet. Dic . . . I would scare th . . . jumped on their . . . the fellows across . . . back the leaders. . . . boats are these?" . . . his, and that one . . . You see Bushnell . . . from the little v . . . across the river. T . . . lows that own th . . . manage them, get . . . a long sharp stick . . . where the cattle st . . . punch them in the . . . them turn—don't . . . back. Now," I say . . . your cattle out of . . .

Their boss says . . . $25 to get us acro . . .

I says, "Fellows, . . . fit to cross. They . . . dition." They was . . . big as my fingers . . . hungry. I said, "Yo . . . when they come o . . . herd back here a c . . .

heard a prayer in all my life touch me like that. I can't tell it yet without crying.

Now why had them mavericks followed all the way from Texas? We tried to drive them back and to cut them out but they wouldn't leave. They wasn't branded and it was against the law to have them in the herd, but we couldn't drive them back. I would not have dared to kill Bushnell's cattle to feed these people. Now I know why the strays had followed all the way, but I could not understand it until then.

We drove on over the mountain and passed the little hill where they had buried them that died. Oh, rows and rows of little graves!

We found more near Yellville in caves, half starved. We left them meat and hardtack; that was all we had.

Not all these women were bushwhackers' wives. Some of them was women who had good homes; their husbands had gone to war. The soldiers burned them out alike. That evening we stopped at an old plantation. No fences, no trees, but rich land that had grown up to grass for the cattle. A girl came out and said we could not camp there.

Old Fred was b-b-b-ing, stuttering so he couldn't say a word when I come up. There she was, a girl, young and pretty, but awful thin and poor. Her eyes was large, and dark all around them.

She said, "You can't stop on this plantation."

Says I, "How far to the next one?" She says, "A wee bit."

I knew this was only a mile or two and I says to the boys, "Go on."

Then I said, "Why are you here alone?"

Says she, "I wouldn't talk to you a minute but for the pin you wear. My father was a Mason, and my oldest brother. They were both killed on the battlefield. The news killed my mother. Then bushwhackers stole all our horses and cattle and even the chickens. They sent home from the war my youngest brother to die: he had gangrene in his foot. Our buildings were burned by the Union soldiers, and I did not have a spade to bury my brother when he died. I dug that grave there with

my hands and covered it with evergreens."

"What are you waiting for?" I asked. "To die."

"But you are a young woman," I said. "You might get away and maybe marry and have a family of your own and live a life yet."

She burst into tears then. All the time she'd been dry-eyed.

"No! No!" she said. "The only man I would marry is dead on the battlefield with my father and brother. We would have been married as soon as the war was over, so I am waiting to die. The only thing that I dread is to die here and have the wild animals eat my body."

I said, "I won't leave you here like this. What the devil do you eat?"

She said that she ate wintergreen berries and wild plums, and rolled stones in front of the cave at night.

Then I said, "I will take you back to these people at the crossroad."

"No!" she said, she would not ride a Yank's horse. Gawd, she had spunk.

Then I said, "You can walk it?"

She said, "Yes," that she had many times.

Then I said, "I will leave you here on only one condition, that you will promise to go to them."

She considered this a long time, then she said she would.

I said, "You look like a girl who will keep your word."

She said, "Yes," that she would go.

I can't tell about them all but there was one widow, made a widow by the war, told of the Yanks burning the house over her sick sister. She asked them to spare the house for her sister's sake, but they carried her out and burned the house. There was not a fruit tree left. They even burned the spring house where the last drink of milk was. She buried her sister with her hands, covered her with boughs and reeds. No wonder these southerners hated the people from the North. We left her hardtack and meat.

Then there was a woman and two boys. Fred said to the boys, "W-w-what do you eat?"

"Oh, we got melons now."

Fred went down to see their house and took them some meat. The woman

put her head out and said not to come any nearer.

Fred asked why.

She said, "I haven't enough clothes to cover my nakedness."

Fred came back and told me. I went down and said, "Lady, would you wear a man's shirt?"

"Yes," she said she would.

"And I have a man's overcoat—you can make a skirt."

She said, "I have nothing to make it with."

So old Fred got out the thread and needles. Bartlett was the smallest man in the lot, so we sent one of his white shirts.

The next day the woman came up in the original hobble skirt, but no woman in a hobble skirt was ever as proud as that woman.

*On August 23, Perry Case and his men crossed over into southern Missouri. Even though they were no more than two weeks' drive away from the Mississippi River and Illinois, their hardships had by no means ended: they had run headlong into a drought area. Creek beds were dry, and water was nowhere to be found. Crossing the Black River, thirsty cattle drank so much that several died. To make matters worse, Perry discovered that the Missouri farmers were openly hostile to cattle drivers.*

We met a man from Illinois. He said, "You are aware that it is unlawful to drive Texas cattle in Missouri, hain't you?"

"No," I said, "I did not know anything about it."

He said some herd had passed through, and from the ground where

the Texas cattle had eaten, the native cattle had took Spanish fever. Should one of the native cattle come in and stop to eat at a spot where the Texas cattle had breathed or left scent of body from over night, they would start to bellow and paw as if they smelt fresh blood. They would then start drooling and staggering, not drink, gnaw roots and the ground about them, and finally fall over dead. Nothing could save them: they had Spanish fever.

That was why they passed the law prohibiting Texas cattle to pass through the state.

There I was. What to do? I didn't think I had more than two or three days' drive in Missouri to the Mississippi, where we could cross into Illinois. If we went back down and crossed the Mississippi from Arkansas, we must also cross the Ohio River. Our money was gone, the boys' clothes gone, the weather getting cool. I didn't want to break their laws, and I was afraid they might take all the cattle if we did. But if we went back to Arkansas and crossed the Mississippi and Ohio it would take much more for the ferry and who could tell what we would run into then.

I rode ahead to Jackson, Missouri, and picked out a way. We waited several days for the cattle to fill well and for the moon to get full so that we would have a moonlight night. I decided to try it.

We started one evening and drove all night and all the next day and the next night. We never stopped the herd. In this time I rode ahead and picked out the trail. I planned to not drive near one of the settlements and had a way picked within seven miles of Jackson. There it was fenced in and we had to drive the road.

When we came to the edge of the prairie seven miles from Jackson at daylight in the morning, the herd had fed two hours and was pretty well filled. At daybreak I knew there would be trouble. I had said, "Boys, we are in the wrong. Don't let's start any of the trouble. We are wrong and are disobeying the laws so we will have to take a little. If there is any shooting let them fire the first shot."

A party of six or eight men came up and before long sixteen men were there. They asked for the owner of the drove. I told them I expected that the owner was dead and I was in charge.

They said, "Did you not know it was against the law to drive Texas cattle through this state?"

"Yes sir, I did."

"Then why the devil are you doing it?"

A horse came up then as fast as his rider could make him ride. Someone said, "That is Squire Ellis."

He stopped short in front of me and said, "I have come to save bloodshed."

Old Fred boiled up, an old soldier in the war, four years. He said, "B-b-by God, we w-w-w-on't be shot down."

I said, "See here, men. I want to tell you about this. I did not come this way just to break your laws, and I don't want to cause anyone any trouble. We started from Ohio, and have been through some tight places. The man who bought these cattle lost his nerve; he was an old man and sick. We sent him home to die. I am taking these cattle through for his widow and family and to get enough to pay these men. We are out of money. Our cattle haven't had salt for weeks. We haven't had enough to eat ourselves. My men all need clothes. They have been through a good deal, and can't stand much more. I did not know you had passed this law until I got here. You made this law since I started. Now we have come fast. Nowhere in Missouri have we stopped where there was settlers until here on the edge of the prairie. None of your cattle are exposed. If you will keep them away from this pasture until a rain or three days of heavy dew, your cattle will not catch the Spanish fever."

One of the riders spurred up his horse and cracked his whip. "That is the damn Yank of it," he said. I shook my head at old Fred and Bartlett. That was hard for soldiers to take.

Ellis said, "You wear a Mason pin. Several of these men are Masons. I will see what I can do." He took the men aside. They parleyed for an hour. Gawd, things looked bad. I did not know what would happen. After all we had been through I thought they might take the cattle. Then Ellis came over and said, "They voted to let you go on with a majority of one. Get out quick before some more come up."

Brethren of the Mystic, I want to say to you here is where my Masonry done me some good. If it hadn't been for that pin no one can tell what would have happened.

I said, "Boys, you know how to get them there in a hurry." I said, "Ellis, there will be more trouble ahead. Can you help us through?"

He said he would, and another said he would help, then another and another until seven of the men volunteered and rode ahead to the town and the mayor. I told him to tell the ferryman we would have to leave ponies to pay for ferriage until we could tensive preparations for the founding of a permanent settlement the following year. The Russians were acting slowly, but with considerable thoroughness and skill. That spring and summer they conducted what was actually a trial run of their colonial plans. Fur hunting continued unabated. A post was set up at the Farallon Islands, a favorite haunt of the fur seal, just off the Golden Gate; and during a four-month period three thousand of the animals were killed. Additional buildings were erected at Bodega, and a crop of wheat was sown, harvested, and carried to Sitka. Counting the Aleuts aboard the half dozen American ships that were present, the Russians had a formidable force of five hundred men on the coast: the total garrison of Spanish California was not much larger.

Thus far open warfare had been avoided, but relations with the Spaniards grew tense. Kuskov decided that Bodega was too exposed to serve as the main Russian base. The rugged terrain north of the Russian River (the Russians named it the Slavianka, "charming little one") seemed more promising. Headlands curved above the gray ocean, and the land fell steeply to the sea in cliffs and deep, wooded gulches. The high coastal plateau was hemmed by a forest of titanic redwoods that extended to Oregon. So secluded is this spot that even now it is thinly populated.

Thirteen miles above the river and thirty above Bodega, Kuskov discovered a safe cove. San Francisco was eighty miles away. The little harbor, fronting on the open sea, was inferior to the enclosed anchorage at Bodega (which in any case Kuskov intended to keep), but it could be used nevertheless. One hundred feet above the water, protected on three sides by the ocean, was a flat tableland where the Pomo Indians had established the village of Mad-Shui-Nui. Kuskov looked no farther. For "three blankets, two axes, three hoes, and a miscellaneous assortment of beads"—some accounts say that three pairs of trousers were also included—he purchased about one thousand acres from the Indians. If the payment seems niggardly, it may be said for Kuskov that this was the only known occasion during the colonial period when the California Indians were given anything at all for their land. The Spaniards did not pay them even beads.

Kuskov wintered in Sitka, but on March 15, 1812—a fateful year in the history of both Europe and America—he was back in California to construct a fort. He laid out a quadrangle about one hundred yards square, its corners corresponding roughly to the cardinal points of the compass; and his force of ninety-five Russians and eighty Aleuts, aided by some local Pomos, went to work.

Huge redwood trees were felled. The logs were hewn into posts and planks; and a stockade commenced to rise. At the northern and southern corners were blockhouses, fitted with cannon ports. These bastions were designed to control all the approaches to the fort. Eventually, when there was a full complement of forty-one guns, the fort did become impregnable to any force the Spaniards could have mustered.

Throughout the spring and summer, work continued on the doughty little fortress, but some portions remained unfinished when Kuskov dedicated the colony with a ceremony on September 11. He named it Rossiya—an ancient name for Russia, which sometimes was written simply as Ross. Usually the establishment was called Fort Ross, the name that has persisted.

*A finger shield, used by Alaska Indians for sewing, was drawn by Langsdorff.*

In the context of world history the dedication of Ross, in its lonely setting of natural grandeur, was an event of minor but poignant significance. The raising of the Czarist standard, to the accompaniment of salutes, prayers, and singing, occurred at a moment when Russia's very survival as an independent nation was in peril. Napoleon occupied Moscow only three days later, and on the day following that, the city was set afire, probably by French looters. It burned for six days; and a month afterward began the dismal retreat westward across the snow.

The colonists endured their first winter in California with great hardship, largely because the Spaniards refused to provide them with food in exchange for cloth and iron they offered to trade. The situation was made worse by the outbreak of war between the United States and Britain; the Yankee ships on which so much depended were soon bottled up in their home ports. But in 1813 the authorities at Monterey relented. Goods and produce valued at $14,000 were exchanged. The Russians received cattle and horses, wheat, beans, dried beef, tallow, and other supplies. Yet they could never count on this commerce. Spanish policy often hardened without warning.

Kuskov, however, did not sit idle. He was handicapped by the inefficiency and laziness of many of his men, the majority of whom were convicts from Siberian penal camps; but he was an enthusiastic builder and farmer, and he drove them as hard as he could. More buildings, including a windmill, were erected at Ross; the installations at Bodega were enlarged and improved; a permanent post was established on the

Farallon Islands. The Aleuts went out regularly in their *bidarkas*. Land was fenced and tilled. A vineyard was started in 1817 with grapevines brought from Peru. Three years later an orchard of one hundred trees—apple, pear, cherry, peach, and bergamot—was planted on an enclosed rise of land some distance from the fort. There was a garden of roses and other flowers.

Slowly the settlement became more comfortable. Women arrived from Alaska; none at first was Russian-born, but some had Russian fathers. There were marriages, and children were born. Population passed two hundred.

Fear of Spanish retaliation declined with each year. The Napoleonic Wars had dealt Spain blows from which she had yet to recover, and her American possessions were moving toward independence. Russia, on the other hand, emerged from the fighting as one of the great victors. One sign of revivified Russian power was the arrival of the brig *Rurik* in San Francisco on October 2, 1816.

Although the vessel was commanded by Lieutenant Otto von Kotzebue of the Russian Navy, and flew the imperial war flag, she ostensibly was bound on a round-the-world voyage of exploration. The expedition had been personally underwritten by Count Rumiantsev, acting as a private individual, for he had retired from office two years earlier. Aboard the *Rurik* were two eminent young scientists: the entomologist Johann Friedrich Eschscholtz, and the naturalist and poet Adelbert von Chamisso.

Yet Kotzebue evidently was more interested in showing the flag in civilized ports than in braving unmapped coasts in the Arctic. He behaved in San Francisco with singular hauteur, insisting for example that the Spaniards salute his ship deferentially with a larger number of guns than was usual. The Spaniards for their part acted with traditional politeness and warm hospitality.

Then Governor Pablo Vincente de Sola arrived from Monterey to demand the immediate abandonment of Ross. Suddenly Kotzebue became amiable. He replied that, although justice seemed clearly on Spain's side, he was without authority to act in the matter, but he would be glad to bring it to the attention of his emperor. Sola (it would seem gratuitously) agreed to refrain from violence against the intruders until the Czar ordered them to leave. More profound developments were taking place which eventually compelled the Russians to leave California. Russia was preoccupied by ambitions in Europe and Asia, but the fate of Ross was actually determined by events in the New World.

Of most immediate importance was the approach-

ing extinction of the sea otter: by 1821 the catches had fallen off so alarmingly that the Czar issued a ukase that barred foreign vessels from the coast north of San Francisco.

Meanwhile the United States had become aroused. To the American people Alexander was the incarnation of political evil. He had lost all trace of his youthful liberalism; instead he stood guilty before the young Republic as the author of the autocratic Holy Alliance—"unholy," Americans called it. Russian provocation is frequently overlooked as one of the main reasons for Monroe's epochal message of December 2, 1823—now known as the Monroe Doctrine—but both the President and Secretary of State John Quincy Adams, as well as the Congress, suspected that the Czar was "occupied with a scheme worthy of his vast ambition . . . the acquisition of the gulf and peninsula of California and of the Spanish claim to North America." It was Rezanov's scheme.

The Americans were not acting selflessly. They were aware that the harbor of San Francisco was, in the words of a secret report received by Congress, "one of the most convenient, extensive, and safe in the world, wholly without defense, and in the neighborhood of a feeble, diffused, and disaffected population." Already some Americans were determined that the magnificent bay should be controlled by no other nation than their own. The Monroe Doctrine made it clear to Russia that she could contemplate no further expansion in the New World without the risk of battle with the American fleet. Thus ended the grandiose plans of Rezanov and Alexander, of Rumiantsev, Baranov, and Kuskov. Within a few years all of them were dead, and the impulse toward colonization—never strong at the Russian court—failed to survive them.

Eighteen years remained to the Russians in California after the Monroe Doctrine was issued in 1823. By paradox this final period was the most pleasant in the history of the colony. As the settlement lost economic and political justification for its continuance, it acquired comforts, such as window glass, which were

*This unusual Kodiak Indian percussion instrument was made of puffin beaks.*

counted as rare luxuries in Spanish California. When the French traveler Bernard Duhaut-Cilly arrived at Bodega on June 3, 1827, he found none of the "rudeness" of the presidios he had visited. Instead, he saw "well-made roofs, houses of elegant form, fields well-sown and surrounded with palisades." The place had a "wholly European air."

Fort Ross, after fifteen years of steady improvement, stood impressively complete. At the north and south rose the turrets of the blockhouses. At the eastern corner was the chapel built in 1823, surmounted by a belfry and a low dome; it was built into the stockade and seems to have been fitted with gun ports, so that it too could be used as a defensive bastion. Diagonally across from the chapel, but standing separate from the walls, was the "fine house" of the commandant. There were seven other buildings within the stockade: officers' quarters, storehouses, a kitchen, and a jail. Discipline was severe at Ross; floggings were administered; and social distinctions between officers and men were strictly enforced.

Outside the walls was the "town." Some fifty structures were scattered among gardens, vineyards, and cultivated fields. Close to the stockade were the "pretty little houses" of the Russian colonists; it is difficult to have a clear idea of them from drawings of the period, all of which disagree in detail. Further away were the "flattened cabins" of the Aleuts and the "cone-shaped huts" of the California Indians. According to Duhaut-Cilly, sixty Russians, eighty Aleuts, and eighty Indians, together with their families, were living at Ross at this time. The total population must have been about four hundred.

Meanwhile, the Spanish *frontera del norte* finally had been extended above the Golden Gate by the establishment of the last two units in the mission chain, at San Rafael (founded in 1817) and Sonoma (1823). As replies to the Russian intrusion in California they were tardy enough, but they did hasten the settlement of modern Marin and Sonoma counties. With the padres came troops and rancheros, who in 1822 became subjects of the new Republic of Mexico. They were led by the great man of the period, Mariano Guadalupe Vallejo. After the missions were secularized by order of the Mexican government—San Rafael in 1833, and Sonoma in 1834—Vallejo's power was unopposed in the region. His splendid feudal hacienda, Casa Grande, which stands in broad fields in the Petaluma valley, was designed to resist further Russian encroachment. The two-story adobe structure, whose continuous open balconies and wide sheltering roofs give it exceptional architectural distinction, was essentially a fortress. It was laid out in a U-plan around a large patio; the walls were four feet thick; and there were caches of arms and defensive earthworks in the surrounding fields. The long northern side faced Ross—only forty miles away. If Vallejo was unable to expel the Russians, although he sometimes dreamed of making the attempt, they certainly lacked the strength to chase him from Casa Grande.

A modus vivendi developed. There was a steady exchange of produce between Ross and Casa Grande. The Russians were permitted to open a commercial agency in Yerba Buena, as the trading station that would become the city of San Francisco was then called. Nevertheless, Ross went into steady financial decline. As the fur trade fell off, expenditures exceeded receipts by five to one.

The later commandants at Ross perceived that the basic wealth of the colony consisted of the immense forests that today comprise the "Redwood Empire," one of the richest stands of timber in the world. They sold what lumber they could in California and Hawaii, but the market was necessarily limited. Shipbuilding was attempted, but the tan oak—unsuitable for this purpose in any case—was used while the wood was green, and the four vessels that were built did not last on the water. The Russian carpenters even prefabricated houses, ingeniously designing them to be assembled without nails; but few of these structures were needed on the coast. During the Gold Rush, ready-made buildings were to be shipped tremendous distances by sea to California. But by then the Russians were gone.

One hope remained for the salvation of the colony. Mexico, which won independence in 1821, was eager to obtain Russian recognition—eager enough to consider making a cession of land in return. The governor of Alaska, the distinguished explorer Ferdinand von Wrangell, hoped that he could thus obtain the lands of the missions at Sonoma and San Rafael, and perhaps the entire territory north of the Golden Gate; but negotiations were fruitless. Wrangell did lay the basis for a commercial treaty, but Czar Nicholas I, whose motto was "orthodoxy, autocracy, and national unity," would not countenance dealings with the upstart republic.

Ross was doomed. The stockholders of the Russian-American Company asked to be relieved of the burden of maintaining the colony, and on April 15, 1839, the Czar approved the decision to withdraw.

Two years were required to close down the settlement. They were spent in an atmosphere that suggests Chekhov's drama *The Cherry Orchard*. The last commandant, Alexander Rotchev, wrote lyric poetry and translated Shakespeare, Schiller, and Victor Hugo into Russian. His wife, the blond young Princess Helena Gagarin, was the most brilliant woman who had yet appeared in California. Vallejo, like everyone else, was captivated by her. She was "a very beautiful lady of twenty Aprils," he wrote with his usual eloquence, "who united to her other gifts an irresistible affability." Even the Indian chief Solano was fascinated by her; and if Vallejo's account can be trusted, he and his

*Liberal as a young man, Czar Alexander I encouraged Russia's colonizing efforts; later he lost interest in them.*

warriors once planned to steal her during a visit that she and her husband made to Sonoma.

The wives of two or three other Russian officers had also come to California, and for the first time Ross lost its masculine somberness. The ladies were elegantly dressed; there were parties and dancing; and the Princess had a glass conservatory—it caused a sensation in California—where she spent happy hours among her plants. A summer house was erected in the fruit orchard—there were nearly three hundred trees now—and when the Rotchevs dined with their guests in the open pavilion, it was hung with the imperial colors. The commandant's house was the only one in California that really pleased a finicky French visitor, Count Eugene Duflot de Mofras, who "appreciated the joy of a choice library, French wines, a piano, and a score of Mozart" when he visited Ross.

At last arrangements were made for evacuation. The Hudson's Bay Company agreed to take over the task of provisioning Sitka; and the ruler of the Sacramento Valley, John Augustus Sutter, purchased the buildings, furnishings, equipment, and stock of the fort for $30,000. The land, to which the Russians had no title in spite of the payment made to the Indians, was not offered for sale. Later it came into the hands of American ranchers.

The Americans were spreading out everywhere in California. They were coming through the passes of the Sierras and by ship around the Horn. When Wrangell passed through Monterey en route to Mexico in 1835, a young sailor before the mast of the *Pilgrim*, Richard Henry Dana, gave him a letter to be forwarded to Boston. Dana's observations of the potential wealth and present defenselessness of California, together with the reports of fellow countrymen who had come west, were public knowledge in the United States. The drive against Mexico had begun. Texas was independent. Soon Frémont and his party would enter California, and it also would be detached from Mexican rule.

The end of the Hispanic era, too, was in sight. Squatters were taking land in the vicinity of Ross and Sonoma. These intruders, who were to stage the Bear Flag Revolt in 1846, simply "would not give up the places occupied by them," complained Lieutenant Dimitri Zavalashin, who conceded that the only choice remaining to the Russians was to fight the Americans or leave. It was the better part of wisdom to depart.

The Russians left early in 1842, and everything movable was transferred from Ross to Sutter's Fort on the Sacramento, including the dismantled buildings. Sutter recalled that Madame Rotchev begged him not to destroy her conservatory. But his men "could not put it together because they did not understand the workmanship of the Russian carpenters."

History moved swiftly in the next decade. In 1848 gold was found at Sutter's Mill, and all Sutter had acquired from the Russians, together with all that he had in the world, was engulfed in the rush for wealth. In 1850 California joined the Union, and a new phase of history began.

Throughout their twenty-nine years at Ross, the Russians had regarded Mount Mayacamas, as the Indians called it, the highest peak in the region. Shortly before their departure Ivan Vosnesensky and Gyorgy Tschernikh climbed to the crest, and named it Mount St. Helena, probably in honor of the reigning Czarina, or the saint whose day it was, rather than in honor of Helena Gagarin. From the summit of this formidable mountain, 4,343 feet above the sea, the Russians looked out over some of the richest and most beautiful country in California: the Napa and Sonoma valleys directly below with their farms, orchards, and vineyards; and to the south, the great sheet of bay, quite silver in the sun. Today the region is dotted with cities and towns. Smoke rises from the industrial plants on the shores of the incomparable harbor. The silver bridge, tiny but distinct, leaps in its great trajectory from Oakland to San Francisco; and there in the sunlit distance rise the towers of the metropolis. All this was at stake when the Russians contended in the great international struggle for California.

---

*A writer on architecture, Allan Temko has been teaching at the University of California at Berkeley. He is presently at work on a history of San Francisco Bay and its culture.*

in every direction. It is a land almost without trees and one completely monotonous to anyone raised among even modest hills, but it is a joy to the farmers who work its deep, rich, stoneless soil.

The effects of the ice on life were profound. It completely annihilated everything unable to get out of its slow-moving way, and when it retreated it left a lifeless desert. However, it is very doubtful that any large expanse of barren debris was exposed at any one time by the melting ice because plants can spread with surprising speed even on unlikely soil, and the retreat of the glacier, only a fraction of a mile a year, was no faster than most plants can follow.

The large mammals associated with the ice age have disappeared, some long ago, a few outlasting all four glaciations. The Kodiak bear of Alaska is a splendid survival but the rest are gone.

One of the most curious of the survivals is an insect, the White Mountain butterfly. It is a creature that can exist only in a cold climate and flourishes today in Labrador. It moved south ahead of the glacier and followed it back north as it melted, all except some which sought refuge from the warming climate by fluttering up mountainsides. Two such colonies survive in the United States. One found a safe haven on the chilly slopes of Mount Washington, New England's highest peak; the other lives on a mountain in Colorado.

Probably the greatest of all effects of the last glacier was that it brought man to North America. Until that time, the Western hemisphere had been, as far as all evidence available to us indicates, empty of humans; with so much water tied up in the icecaps, ocean levels dropped three to four hundred feet to make the Bering Strait a dry and easy passage for nomads from Asia. The first comers very likely were restricted to the Arctic at first, prevented by the ice from moving south. Strange though it may seem, the northern two thirds of Alaska was free of ice except on the mountains, while at the same time the Arctic Ocean was unfrozen. Though hardly balmy, the region was much milder than it is today, and artifacts found along the northern seashore indicate that man tarried there until the glaciation had passed its peak and a way had opened to the south.

But once started, the immigrants came fast. Charred bones of an extinct bison, associated with arrowheads and indicating a feast after a successful hunt, have been found in Clovis, New Mexico; radioactive carbon dating gives their age as approximately 9,900 years. Much more surprising was the debris from an-

other site, the burned bones of a sloth and an extinct horse uncovered near the Strait of Magellan, about as far from the Bering Strait as it is possible to get. Carbon 14 dating established that this meal was eaten nine thousand years ago. The glacier reached its southern limit eleven thousand years ago, and if we accept the idea that man did not find a way south until somewhat later, it means that human beings made their way over rivers and mountains and through jungles from Alaska to the limits of South America in less than two thousand years.

Since the Northern hemisphere has had four separate glaciations in recent geological times, the inevitable question is whether we can expect a fifth. The answer appears to be in the affirmative.

Until recently, attempts to explain the recurring times of ice have assumed a temporary cooling of the earth's climate for one reason or another. None of these theories has quite explained all the facts. Within the past several years, however, a new theory has been advanced and has gained wide acceptance. Its authors are Maurice Ewing, a geophysicist at Columbia University, and William Donn, a geologist-meteorologist; their argument is that glacial periods result from periodic warming of the Arctic Ocean.

The Arctic Ocean, they point out, is a sea almost separate from the other waters of the earth. Its connection with the Pacific at the Bering Strait is so narrow and shallow it allows no significant interchange of waters. The passage between the Arctic and the North Atlantic is broader, but across its bottom, between Norway and Greenland, extends a shallow sill, less than three hundred feet deep in most places.

The currents flowing across the sill bring warm Atlantic water into the polar sea, and although the net gain each year is tiny, over thousands of years it is enough to make the Arctic Ocean very much warmer. As a result, the ice on the water becomes thinner, patches of open water grow larger, and eventually the time comes when the ocean is completely free of ice.

A polar sea without ice opens a new stage in the glacial cycle. The warm, open water gives off a great deal of water vapor by evaporation; the moisture is swept south and overland by the winds where it cools off and falls as rain or snow. The open Arctic is such a prolific producer of precipitation that the increased winter snowfall amounts to more than the oblique rays of the sun can melt away during the short northern summer. The snow accumulates and packs into ice until, after tens of thousands of years, the icecap has become two miles or so thick. The day comes when the tremendous pressure begins to push the ice outward and another continental glacier is on its way.

But even as they form, icecaps carry the mechanism for their own destruction—according to the Ewing-Donn theory. With so much moisture becoming locked up in ice, ocean levels slowly drop until the Bering Strait becomes dry land and the flow over the Norway-Greenland sill becomes greatly restricted, so that not enough warm water can flow into the polar ocean to keep it from freezing. The Arctic Ocean cools off and finally freezes over again. Since very little moisture evaporates from ice, the snowfalls become much lighter—and far to the south the glacier front comes to a stop.

Once again the situation is changed. With snowfall reduced, the glacier is not replenished at the old rate, and so begins to shrink. Water from the melting ice makes the oceans rise, only a fraction of an inch a year but, in the fullness of time, enough to let the currents increase their flow over the northern sill, bringing ever more warm water into the gelid Arctic.

In this year 1960 A.D., we are (still according to the Ewing-Donn theory) at the point in the cycle where the Arctic Ocean is almost ready to shed its old, old, covering of ice. The north-polar ice is going very fast; it covers twelve per cent less area and is forty per cent thinner than it was only fifteen years ago. At that rate it could disappear completely in less than a human lifetime, although we cannot say whether this is a normal climate fluctuation or a steady trend.

But even making allowances, the beginning of the next glacial era might still be breathing down our necks. Eventually the ice will pile up high enough to begin pushing outward from its own weight and will make its slow but inevitable way into the United States again. How long will it be? Much time and study and additional evidence will be necessary before even an informed guess can be made. But we do know one thing: the beginnings will be completely undramatic. Winter snowfalls will increase, so that at the end of the summer some snow will still linger in the tundra lands of northern Canada, probably nothing more than a few patches of slush in the shade of rocks and hummocks of moss. The next autumn the bits of slush will be just a little larger and deeper when the freeze-up comes.

Only a few Eskimos and scientists will notice.

*Ralph K. Andrist, who is now engaged in promotion for a religious organization, has been a magazine editor, radio newsman, publicist, and college instructor. He has also written documentary radio programs which draw heavily on the history of the Minnesota region for their background.*

## Did the North Pole Wander?

What caused the ice ages? Why were the Siberian mammoths frozen alive, or how did great forests grow in Antarctica? The theory propounded by Maurice Ewing and William Donn, and described by Mr. Andrist in his article, is only one of the most rigorous and ingenious of many attempts to account for the often-contradictory evidence left behind by the glaciers. As recently as 1953 a geologist called this "one of the greatest riddles in geological history."

Some investigators have argued for a change in the amount of heat received from the sun, either by a shift in the earth's position or the interference of some cosmic dust cloud. And some, with much data to support them, have suggested that the poles may not always have been located where we find them now. Studies of ancient rocks have shown that many (those older than sixty million years) are permanently magnetized in a very different direction from the present poles, reinforcing the theory that the land masses on the earth's surface—slowly, during millions of years—may change their positions.

One of the most unorthodox proposals is that of Charles H. Hapgood, who maintains in his book *Earth's Shifting Crust* (1958), that the surface may have moved even in more recent times, shifting the poles, causing the last icecap over North America to melt, and bringing down the freezing cold on Siberia. What the globe would have looked like earlier—if the pole had until then been situated in the region of Hudson Bay, as Mr. Hapgood believes—is shown in the sketch below. His theory is by no means accepted scientifically, but his vigorous defense of it serves to remind us how many puzzles are buried in the past, and are yet to be solved.

—*The Editors*

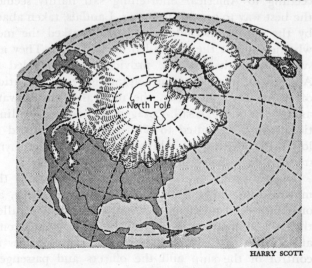

HARRY SCOTT

# The Revolution's Caine Mutiny CONTINUED FROM PAGE 13

the initial voyage, they had insured a supply of fresh meat for the long journey by purchasing sows with their own funds. Naturally they considered the swine their own property. But Landais demanded one half of the pigs because he owned the boar that begot them; on that ground he ordered the officers to refrain from killing any of them without his permission.

On the trip back to America the Captain became steadily more abusive and was so tactless as to reprimand his officers before the crew. On the night of July 13, Landais appeared on the quarter-deck and gave the ship's first officer, Lieutenant J. A. Degge, a public dressing-down for not keeping the ship reared to the wind. Hitherto Degge had been one of Landais' most loyal supporters. Now, unable to stomach any more abuse, he shouted to the men to cut off all the weather braces. Landais took exception to the tone of his voice and ordered him below. Degge refused to go.

"I had rather be in hell," Degge was later quoted as saying, "than to sail with a man I cannot please."

A slapstick scene followed, with Landais chasing Degge up the gangway. The Frenchman called upon Captain Parke of the Marines to arrest the Lieutenant, but Degge armed himself, went into the wardroom, and stayed below.

With passengers, officers, and crew completely against the Captain, a series of crises was building up. The first occurred on the morning of August 5, when virtually the whole ship's company—a mixture of Americans, Frenchmen, Scots, and several other nationalities—came to the quarter-deck and asked the Captain why, since the wind was fair that morning, he had ordered sail taken up. Why was he not proceeding to America? Shortening sail hardly seemed the best way to get to the Banks. Landais, taken aback by the defiant attitude of the crew, asked the men whether or not they intended to obey him. They answered that they would, provided he proceeded to America at once. Since the Captain gave no indication of giving such an order, the men all went forward and began to make sail. Enraged at their insubordination, Landais shouted to Third Lieutenant Lynd to lower the fore-topsail, which had been hoisted. Lynd tried to do so, but the crew would not let him.

Then Landais had no recourse but to order the marines put under arms at once. Captain Parke, an original and consistent anti-Landais stalwart, called the roll of marines. Not a single man would come aft. A state of mutiny now existed, with the crew in control of the ship and the officers and passengers

exceedingly uneasy. Here Landais' indecisiveness was fatal. All witnesses at the trial agreed that had Landais called upon his officers at this time he would have had their support, and the crew might possibly have been overawed. One of the officers named Buckley went to the Captain and asked him, "in the name of God," what to do when so many were against him. Landais did not know the answer. He went below, allowing the crew to make sail and take charge of the ship.

The next day, at 10 A.M., the *Alliance* found bottom in thirty-five fathoms on the Banks of Newfoundland. In accordance with regulations laid down by the Continental Congress, the crew were provided with fishing tackle so they could supplement the ship's rations with fresh fish. The men threw their lines overboard and almost at once three fish were caught. Thoroughly beside himself, Landais rushed to the quarter-deck and out of sheer perversity ordered the fish thrown back into the sea and told the officer of the watch to make sail and bear away. This order was carried out, amidst much grumbling.

The fishing episode revealed that Landais could be both spiteful and sadistic. That evening at dinner Samuel Guild, the ship's surgeon, remonstrated with him, pointing out that the stores for the sick were almost expended and that a number of them (three had already died during the passage) needed nourishing food.

"Everybody is in a hurry to get home," Landais retorted, "so everybody will soon be where he can get everything he wants." Furthermore, he argued, if the men stopped to fish they would delay the trip and thus consume more of the precious stores. The surgeon pointed out how ridiculous this argument was: off the Grand Banks the crew needed just two hours to catch a supply sufficient for the remainder of the voyage. Landais replied curtly: "I can stop for nothing."

The reader of *The Caine Mutiny* will recall how Queeg found excuses in migraine headaches and kept to his cabin completely, leaving the running of the ship to his executive officer. Landais did the same. He returned to his cabin, said he was sick, threw himself on his cot, and feigned sleep.

The officers of the *Alliance* now had the greatest difficulty in getting the crew to return to their duty. Accordingly, they requested Landais to head for the nearest port in the United States. He refused, insisting that his orders were to go to Philadelphia. Muttering increased. At 2 P.M. on August 10, two of the foremastmen, Thomas Bayle and James Pratt, proposed to the officers that they change the ship's course to Boston. When the officers refused, the greater part of the ship's company assembled on deck at 3:10 P.M., and when the officers still refused to change course, declared "they would not fire a single broadside against any frigate that they should fall in with if the ship would not carry them to Boston." They warned the officers that they carried nails in their pockets with which to spike the guns should a hostile ship come alongside. During this mutinous altercation Landais did not appear on deck.

At five the next morning the officers drew up a written report on the dangerous condition of the ship and brought it down to Landais, who would not allow the paper to be read. "I will not hear it! I will not hear it!" he cried out. "I have my orders to go to Philadelphia and will go there."

"We now looked upon the Captain as deserting his command," the purser later testified, and Lieutenant Lynd backed him up: "We thought the Captain had abdicated the command and would not assist us and that it was high time to choose somebody to command." The officers then wrote out and signed a statement pointing out the "alarming situation" aboard the frigate "from the discontent of the people which is now of the most serious nature, being universal and fermented to a great degree," but Landais refused to receive the communication, outshouting the delegation and declaring he would neither have nor receive anything from his officers.

The officers now held a meeting and, according to Captain Parke's later testimony at Landais' trial, declared "they would rather be hanged for bringing the ship into a safe port than be taken by an inferior force and carried to the enemy's port." The passengers then submitted to the officers, in writing, their opinion that an officer be designated to conduct the ship to the first safe port in the United States.

Acting with considerable circumspection and with every caution to keep a record of every move they made, the officers by unanimous vote chose Lieutenant Degge to take over the command. Degge was the only commissioned officer aboard except Landais, and he was still under arrest. With understandable reluctance he accepted, but only after the ship's other officers gave him their orders in writing.

"I never saw Captain Landais out of his cabin after that time until we came in sight of land," the purser later told the court.

When the *Alliance* reached Boston, the Navy Board for the Eastern District directed Parke to deliver a letter ordering Landais to leave the ship and to turn over his cabin and furniture to Captain John Barry,

the new commander. When Parke tried to carry out the order, Landais threatened to blow his brains out. Finally, a sergeant and two men had to go in and haul the Captain off the ship.

Landais at once filed formal charges of mutiny by the officers and passengers. "Before God! Bring to light the truth," Landais implored the Navy Board, warning them that the officers were supported in their mutinous behavior by the passengers. "You will find them out but there are very cunning ones among them," he pointed out in a self-revealing sentence. The Board of Admiralty instructed the Navy Board in Boston to hold a court of inquiry into Landais' conduct "from the time he entered on board the *Alliance* at Port L'Orient until her arrival in Massachusetts Bay." In addition to suspending Landais, the commissioners directed the board to determine the ringleaders of the "mutiny" and confine them for court-martial.

As a result of these orders two courts-martial were held: the first, beginning late in November, 1780, inquired into Landais' behavior; the second in January, 1781, tried Lieutenant Degge for mutiny. Presiding over both trials was the naval hero Captain John Barry, whose greatest victories still lay ahead. Two other captains, Samuel Nicholson (who was fiercely jealous of Jones) and Hoystead Hacker, along

CULVER SERVICE

*Faced with a defiant Landais, Jones sought backing from the American commissioners (above). Franklin (center) told him: "If you had stayed on board where your duty lay, instead of coming to Paris, you would not have lost your ship."*

89

with three lieutenants, made up the Landais court. Thomas Dawes, Jr., served as judge advocate. In Degge's trial Henry Johnson was added to the court, and in addition to three naval lieutenants, a lieutenant of the Marines was put on the panel. Neither of the accused men had an attorney. Landais cross-examined the government's witnesses.

The crucial issue at Landais' trial was his mental condition.

"Did you ever see me destitute of any of the common sense such as what I had formerly used to exercise?" Landais asked Lieutenant Lynd.

"When you acted in your own station as commander of the ship I thought you in your proper senses."

"Did you ever see anything that looked like craziness since the command of the ship was taken from me?"

"No."

A more prudent cross-examiner would have stopped here. But Landais plunged recklessly ahead.

"Did you ever hear anyone else say so?" he asked.

"I have heard some of the people say that you were not right," Lynd replied. "I have heard numbers, officers, passengers, and many others say that they did not think you in your proper senses."

Of course, Captain Parke of the Marines had no reason to love Landais, and on the stand he did not beat about the bush. On direct examination, in reply to a question of whether Landais was in his proper senses after leaving L'Orient, he stated: "There were times when I thought he was not." Fitch Poole, captain's clerk on the *Alliance,* testified that the Captain on the last voyage was not himself and that he used to pace his cabin for hours talking to himself.

On the question of whether the supplanting of Landais was carried out in a mutinous spirit, James Warner, a lieutenant of Marines, was explicit. "I looked upon it as absolutely necessary from circumstances."

"Did you not look upon it as a mutiny?"

"No."

The testimony was all in, the judge advocate gave his closing argument, and now Captain Barry summed up the evidence. He found that Landais had been explicitly ordered by Congress to obey Franklin's instructions upon his arrival in France; that in seizing the *Alliance* he had acted directly contrary to these orders; and that he had either permitted or connived at the shipping of private cargoes to America aboard the *Alliance.* Barry was unwilling to discredit the testimony of so many witnesses concerning the events on shipboard: "That every action of theirs to him should be diabolic and every action of his to them

divine is a phenomenon, and to believe such things requires a great share of credulity." Barry went on:

It may be urged again that all were against him and that he had not the confidence of his officers. But is this to his credit? Which is the most probable: that such a number of various characters should without motive conspire to ruin their commander, or that a commander should have some weak part, some alloy in his constitution and by his behavior create enemies? . . .

Barry castigated Landais for reprimanding his officers in the presence of the men. Had the Captain possessed a sense of humor, the presiding judge pointed out dryly, he might have kept the "affair of the pigs and the water" from burgeoning into raging disputes. But Landais' failure to allow his officers and crew to fish could not be so lightly dismissed, Barry insisted. All Landais could have possibly gained by denying such permission was "to get half an hour sooner to America." This hardly justified putting the ship into an uproar and disobeying a resolve of Congress. Barry referred to the court the question whether Landais' conduct "abated or inflamed sedition."

The summation treated at some length Landais' refusal to deliver over his cabin and furniture to Barry himself as the newly appointed commander. As for Landais' refusal to read a letter from the Navy Board delivered by the hand of Captain Parke, Barry observed that "to be obliged to receive it from Captain Parke, of all men in the world an officer whom the captain could never stomach, with whom he had the first quarrel that happened on board and with whom he was now like to have the last—I say for Captain Parke to serve the death warrant, as it were, upon the unfortunate Captain Landais is a circumstance which must excuse, if not justify" his behavior in the matter.

The verdict of the court was a foregone conclusion. By unanimous opinion Pierre Landais was adjudged guilty of a breach of "the orders of the Congress" and of the Navy Board in coming away with the *Alliance* without the permission of Benjamin Franklin. However, since he had acted on the advice of Arthur Lee, "a gentleman learned in the laws and high in office," this could be considered a mitigating circumstance. Landais was found guilty on a second count of a breach of the order of Congress and the Navy Board in "suffering" private goods to be transported on the *Alliance.* Thirdly, he was found guilty of a breach of the first and thirty-seventh articles of the Navy Rules "in not exerting his utmost abilities" to inspect the behavior of passengers, officers, and crew, in not punishing offenders aboard ship, and in not setting a proper example to his officers by the

*The* Alliance, *Massachusetts-built and named for the French-American entente, was a square-rigger with thirty-six guns.*

discharge of duty. Fourthly, he was held guilty of a breach of the order of the Navy Board in not delivering up the ship *Alliance,* her cabin, and cabin furniture. But the court took into consideration the fact that Landais was without money or credit when he landed in Boston, had no comfortable place to lodge except the ship, and that he had "greatly suffered from a mutinous disposition in both passengers and officers and from a real mutiny in the crew." He was sentenced "to be broke and rendered incapable of serving in the American navy for the future."

But if Landais, unlike Queeg, was not permitted to finish his naval career in an obscure naval depot, Lieutenant Degge was not even allowed the ignominy of being assigned to command a Revolutionary version of an LCI. For him there was no technical vindication by a verdict of acquittal. The fact is that in view of the stern code of the sea then prevailing, Degge was a very lucky man indeed. The judges at his court-martial were divided. Captains Barry and Nicholson voted for the death penalty, but the majority view prevailed. Degge was "broke, cashiered, and rendered incapable of serving in the American navy in the future."

Thus for the captain and first officer of the *Alliance* the outcome of the trials was far more conclusive than for the parallel pair on the *Caine,* and the two ships pursued divergent courses once the trials were out of the way. The decrepit mine sweeper *Caine,* accumulating rust and barnacles, continued to serve as a plodding escort vessel, sweeping only six mines throughout the whole of World War II, and in the end was broken up for scrap. For the *Alliance,* her moments of glory lay ahead. The two trials aboard ship had hardly come to an end when the *Alliance* raised sail with Captain Barry on the quarter-deck.

En route to France she captured the privateer *Alert.* Then, leaving L'Orient in company with the forty-gun letter-of-marque ship *Marquis de Lafayette,* she captured the privateers *Mars* and *Minerva* and, following an especially spirited engagement, forced two British brigs, the *Atalanta* and the *Trepassey,* to strike. Finally, to the *Alliance* and Captain Barry must go the distinction of having fought (save for some privateering exploits) the last naval action of the war. In March, 1783, one month before the peace treaty was ratified by Congress, she defeated—but failed to capture—the British ship *Sybil.*

And there were still other mutinies to be recorded on the log of the *Alliance.* On his initial cruise on Landais' ship Barry was forced to report: "I believe a ship never put to sea in a worse condition as to seamen." For disobeying orders under fire three sailors were tried for a breach of the twenty-ninth article of the Navy Rules which fixed the penalty for desertion and cowardice. One of the accused was sentenced to receive 354 lashes on the bare back; the second to wear a halter across his neck and to receive fifty lashes; and the third to "be hanged by the starboard foreyard arm of the said ship *Alliance* until he is dead." But the sentences were never carried out. John Brown, secretary to the Agent of Marine, visited Boston some months after the trials and reported finding the three men in prison awaiting execution of their sentences and suffering acutely from the cold. To "save expense" Brown had two of the culprits whipped and put aboard the frigate *Deane;* the third was sold by the sheriff to pay his bill for fees and board. As Brown reported to Robert Morris, then Agent of Marine, "with the surplus of the money" he procured three good seamen for the *Deane.*

The following year, when the *Alliance* was in the port of New London, the crew mutinied, calling for "liberty and back allowance." Barry, who was on shore at the time, returned to hold an inquiry aboard ship. Three men were court-martialed and flogged.

So from first to last the *Alliance* kept the Navy Boards and courts-martial busy investigating complaints against her officers and men, and the taint of the distraught Landais and his mutinous crew clung to her till the end.

---

*Richard B. Morris is Gouverneur Morris Professor of History and chairman of the history department at Columbia University. Among his books are* The American Revolution: A Brief History; Alexander Hamilton and the Founding of the Nation; *and (with Henry Steele Commager)* The Spirit of 'Seventy-Six. *Professor Morris is now directing the John Jay Papers project and conducting research into the peace settlement that ended the Revolution.*

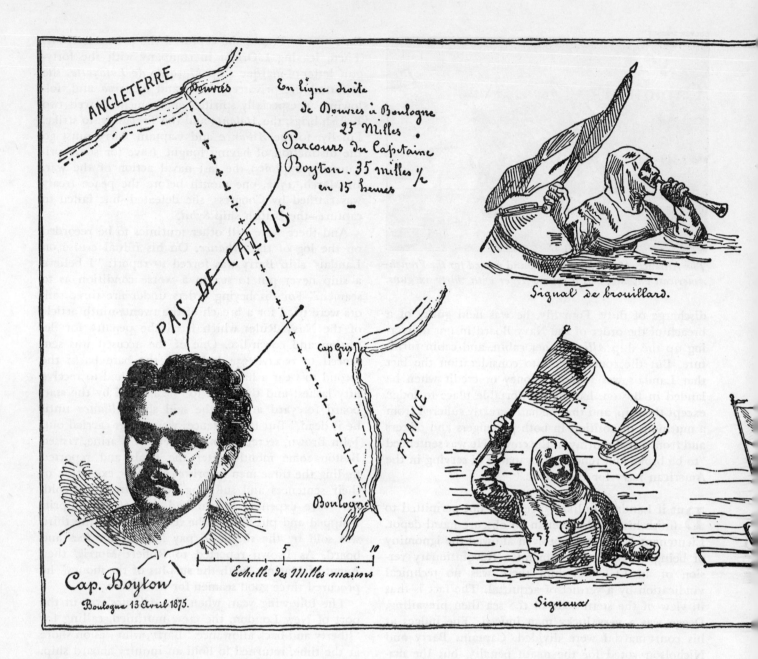

ANGLETERRE

Douvres

En ligne droite
de Douvres à Boulogne
25 Milles
Parcours du Capitaine
Boyton. 35 milles ½
en 15 heures

PAS DE CALAIS

Cap Gris Nez

FRANCE

Boulogne

Cap. Boyton
Boulogne 13 Avril 1875.

5        10
Echelle des Milles marins

Signal de brouillard.

Signaux.

# The Fearless Frogman

CONTINUED FROM PAGE 39

sailor flourished a cutlass at him, but Boyton brushed that aside, too. An excited jabber, everyone talking at once, and then the English officers were convinced there had been no serious mischief, intended or done. Boyton joined his party, and Connors pulled for shore, his passengers severally singing "Merrily We Roll Along" and "Rule, Britannia."

But still the Royal Navy was suspicious. The launch pursued the boat to the wharf, and the bluejackets essayed a landing. Once again they were frustrated. For now they were confronted by a red-shirted con-

stable with a don't-care mustache; this bravo's name was Keiley; he produced a nickel-plated pistol that might have harmed a chicken and, in a fruity brogue, announced: "I don't want any gang of Englishmen pointing guns at Staten Island." A man named Keiley was all the bluejackets needed; they withdrew in confusion.

The publicity from this and similar exploits guaranteed Boyton all the promotion he needed when, a little later, he put together an aquatic circus and toured the country offering exhibitions. For by the time he was in his forties, his urge to risk his life had abated; he was content to display his juggling sea lions, his water races, his high divers, and sit back while the money rolled in. He invented a watery thrill

## Captain Boyton Attempts to Swim the Channel

*A French newspaper published these drawings of Boyton's attempt in April, 1875, to cross the English Channel between Dover and Boulogne. Bad weather forced him to give up a few miles off Cape Gris-Nez, but in May he crossed successfully—in the other direction—in 24 hours.*

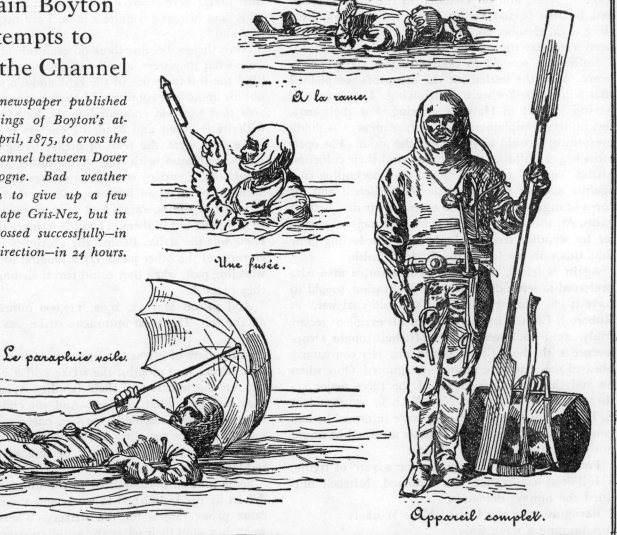

*À la rame.*

*Une fusée.*

*Le parapluie voile.*

*Appareil complet.*

for his customers, too: the Shoot-the-Chutes, a toboggan slide in flat-bottomed boats down a long incline, and splash! into a lagoon; his royalties from this contrivance insured him a comfortable old age.

With the twentieth century, the nineteenth's darling slipped into obscurity, lingering until 1924, an affable man of leisure living in Sheepshead Bay on Long Island, near New York, and occasionally taking off on long Caribbean cruises. Had he accomplished anything by his daredevil exploits? His celebrated rubber suit was forgotten; it was never deemed practical as a safety device on ocean-going steamers. His name was forgotten; and a generation was arising whose feats in and under the water as well would

make Boyton's seem trifling by comparison. And yet, after all, Paul Boyton has his lasting consequence. For, more than any other man, he led a nation to water and made them swim. America was just beginning to want to play and sport outdoors when Boyton appeared, and he became a kind of Pied Piper whose influence in popularizing water sports was incalculable. If not in technique, at least spiritually he was the precursor of the frogmen and the skin-divers and water-skiers who slip so smoothly through the seas today. Paul Boyton was the first to dare the waters.

*Peter Lyon, a free-lance writer living in New York City, has contributed several articles to this magazine, and is a co-author of* The American Heritage Book of the Pioneer Spirit.

wage increase, and on October 29 the miners, mollified by this partial victory, returned to work. Ever since then, October 29, known as "Mitchell Day," has been a holiday throughout the anthracite.

Both sides seemed to realize that it was a phony peace. After the settlement the operators complained that wildcat strikes were multiplying. They regretted having yielded to Hanna's coaxing. For their part, the miners complained that management was doing everything it could to stamp out the union. The operators began building stockades around their collieries, hiring "coalies" to guard them, and stockpiling coal against another strike. Meanwhile, Mitchell and his corps of organizers sought to extend their membership gains. All through the mine fields, the stage was being set for another test; on both sides the feeling grew that this one would be fought to a finish.

Again Mitchell, an innately conservative man who preferred to settle differences by arbitration, sought to stave it off. Throughout 1901 "the cold coal war," as Robert J. Cornell has called it in his excellent recent study, went on. Several times Mitchell sought a conference with the railroad presidents. His courteously phrased requests were refused—or ignored. Once when he and the union presidents of the three major anthracite districts went to New York to see President E. B. Thomas of the Erie, they were informed he had gone to Europe, and when Thomas returned he would not even answer Mitchell's letters.

Finally, in March of 1902, after a year of trying, a full-dress conference was arranged. Mitchell outlined the union's demands:

Recognition of the United Mine Workers
A minimum wage scale
An eight-hour day
A twenty per cent wage increase
The weighing of coal using as the legal ton 2,240 pounds, for which the minimum rate would be sixty cents.

The operators replied that granting these demands would drive some of them into bankruptcy, and negotiations dragged on without practical result, except to postpone a strike that now seemed inevitable.

And yet, looking back, one has the distinct impression that it was not.

One of the operators remarked after the conference that he "did not know but what it was the best thing to do—to make a contract with Mr. Mitchell's organization"; Mitchell, he said, had impressed him "with being a very fair and conservative man." Another said: "I am not prepared to go that far, but I will say

this: that I have changed my mind on several points. This man Mitchell is quite a man. I am beginning to like him."

Nevertheless, because those on each side of the table were what they were, a strike became a certainty. Behind the intransigence of the rank-and-file miner was not his immediate condition (though by modern standards that was bad enough) but the long, hard past, with its crippled and dead, its endless grubbing to make ends meet, the years of dreary living in dreary company houses with the debts piling up at the "pluck-me" company store. The miners held the firm opinion, based upon hard experience, that whatever concessions the operators had ever granted had had to be wrung out of them. The only wringer the miners knew was the strike. Behind the obstinacy of the operators, on the other hand, lay a longing for the free-wheeling past, when they could run their businesses as they pleased.

And so, on May 12, 1902, 147,000 miners walked off the job. The great anthracite strike was on.

As the days of idleness mounted into weeks and the weeks into months, the strike laid a heavy burden on the miners and their families. What savings they had were soon used up. And yet children had to be fed, and household expenses, pared to the minimum, could be pared no further. Nerves frayed, tempers flared easily, and crowds of idle men turned suddenly ugly.

Some miners, uncommitted to the union or simply driven by need, returned to work, and these soon became prime targets for the strikers. Wherever they went they—and their wives and children—were taunted by cries of "Scab!" Some were even set upon by mobs, and a few were killed. One man awoke in the middle of the night to find his house on fire; outside was an angry mob calling for him to be shot. He barely escaped with his life.

When the Reverend Carl Hauser, a Lutheran minister, went to Lansford to conduct burial services for one of his foreign-born parishioners, he was met by a committee and told he should not bury the man, because he was a scab. "He is a Lutheran," Mr. Hauser answered, "he is a Christian and belongs to my church, and I am called by the Lutheran people . . . to bury that man and I will bury that man." But nobody would even go into the house to carry the corpse to the hearse. When finally the minister managed to corral four reluctant pallbearers, they emerged from the house to find an angry crowd—"they were not so-called foreigners but were American people," Mr. Hauser noted—lining both sides of the street and yelling: "Let that dog lie. Bury somebody else," and, "It's a shame to bury a scab." When the lonely little funeral cortege reached the cemetery, more strikers lined the fence. "Nobody went to the grave," Mr. Hauser recalled later, "only the undertaker and a few women, I guess. I went back and before the big crowd I told the sexton, 'You are responsible for that body.'" He was afraid they might desecrate the grave.

Pent-up emotions finally came to a head on July 30 in the town of Shenandoah. Deputy Sheriff Thomas Beddall, escorting two nonunion men, was surrounded by a crowd of five thousand strikers and forced to take refuge in the Reading Railroad depot. When Beddall's brother Joseph attempted to get arms and ammunition to the beleaguered men, he was mobbed and beaten to death. The sheriff managed somehow to escape and to wire Pennsylvania's Governor William A. Stone to send troops into the region to restore order. Next morning two regiments of National Guard infantry and a troop of cavalry under the command of Brigadier General John P. S. Gobin marched into Shenandoah.

Through August the strike dragged on, with no end in sight. The presence of so many soldiers patrolling the streets, as well as the large number of

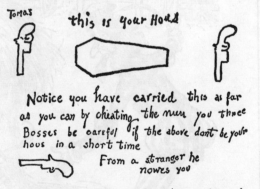

"Coffin-notices" were a favorite weapon of the Molly Maguires, a lawless element that terrorized the coal fields after the Civil War and helped discredit legitimate unions.

armed coal and iron police, grated on the nerves of men and women whose morale was already sagging from long weeks of want. The scattered violence increased, and on August 29 General Gobin felt compelled to issue an order to his unit commanders which concluded:

In moving troops, place reliable, competent and skilled marksmen on the flanks of the command and arm your file closers with loaded guns, and instruct them that in case of attack upon the columns by stones or missiles, where the attacking party cannot be reached, the men thus selected shall carefully note the man attacking the columns, and being certain of his man, fire upon him without any further orders.

To union sympathizers it was soon known as the "shoot-to-kill" order—though in fact the soldiers killed no one—and it made the mood of the strikers even uglier. With the strike going into its fourth month, their morale was at its lowest ebb. Early in August Mitchell himself had doubts; long afterward he recalled: "I am fully convinced that the strike would have collapsed had the operators at this time opened their mines and invited the strikers to return."

But they did not. Instead, just at this juncture their principal spokesman made the greatest tactical blunder of the strike. Back in July a Wilkes-Barre photographer named William F. Clark had written to George F. Baer, president of the Reading, asking him to settle the strike. Clark hoped, he wrote, that God would "send the Holy Spirit to reason in your heart." Baer's answer, which for some reason did not become generally known until August, has become a classic example of capitalistic arrogance at its apogee:

My dear Mr. Clark:
I have your letter of the 16th inst. I do not know who you are. I see that you are a religious man; but you are evidently biased in favor of the right of the workingman to control a business in which he has no other interest than to secure fair wages for the work he does.
I beg of you not to be discouraged. The rights and interests of the laboring man will be protected and cared for—not by the labor agitators, but by the Christian men of property to whom God has given control of the property rights of the country, and upon the successful management of which so much depends. Do not be discouraged. Pray earnestly that right may triumph, always remembering that the Lord God Omnipotent still reigns, and that His reign is one of law and order, and not of violence and crime.

The newspapers of the country, which already favored the strikers, had a field day. "A good many people think they superintend the earth," said The New York Times dryly, "but not many have the egregious vanity to describe themselves as its managing directors." From then on public opinion was almost unanimously on the side of the miners.

Meanwhile autumn was at hand, and in great cities coal supplies were dwindling dangerously. Even President Theodore Roosevelt was worried. He had been worried, in fact, for some time. As early as June 27, he had asked Attorney General Philander Chase Knox if there was any way in which the federal government could intervene. Did the coal and railroad companies constitute a combination in restraint of trade liable to prosecution under the Sherman Act? The statute was too vague, Knox had answered. As Mayor Low of New York City and other local officials communicated to Washington their fears of the consequences of a continued fuel shortage, Roosevelt wrote to Robert Bacon of J. P. Morgan and Company: "The situation is bad, especially because it is possible it may grow infinitely worse. If when the severe weather comes on there is a coal famine I dread to think of the suffering, in parts of our great cities especially, and I fear there will be fuel riots of as bad a type as any bread riots we have ever seen."

He was not oblivious to the political effect of the strike, either. Anthracite, which normally retailed for five or six dollars a ton, was up to twenty dollars in New York, and from Massachusetts, Senator Henry Cabot Lodge was warning the President that factors like this could defeat the Republican party in the forthcoming congressional elections. At least, Roosevelt decided, he would do what he could. He dispatched telegrams to Mitchell and to the principal representatives of the operators, asking them to confer with him in Washington on the morning of October 3.

The meeting was held at No. 22 Lafayette Square, for the White House was undergoing repairs. At one end of the room were Baer and the other coal operators; Attorney General Knox; Roosevelt's secretary, George B. Cortelyou; and Carroll D. Wright, Commissioner of Labor. At the other end were Mitchell and the presidents of the three United Mine Workers anthracite districts. A few seconds after 11 A.M. the President entered the room in a wheelchair—he had been injured in a traffic accident the month before—and launched at once into an earnest appeal for peace. Disclaiming any legal right to intervene, he asked both parties whether they had considered the interests of a third—the public. He went on to detail the horrors of a winter coal famine and concluded: "With all the earnestness there is in me I ask that there be an immediate resumption of operations in the coal mines in some such way as will, without a day's unnecessary delay, meet the crying needs of the people. I appeal to your patriotism, to the spirit that sinks personal consideration and makes individual sacrifices for the general good."

Mitchell was on his feet immediately. "I am much pleased, Mr. President, with what you say. We are willing that you shall name a tribunal which shall determine the issues that have resulted in the strike; and if the gentlemen representing the operators will accept the award or decision of such a tribunal, the miners will willingly accept it, even if it be against our claims."

Baer quickly demonstrated an attitude that showed that his famous "divine right" letter had not been a temporary lapse of common sense. To the President of the United States, his tone was almost as condescending as to the obscure Wilkes-Barre photographer: "Thousands of other workmen are deterred from working by the intimidation, violence, and crime inaugurated by the United Mine Workers, over whom John Mitchell, whom you have invited to meet you, is chief." John Markle, representing the independent operators, asked Roosevelt bluntly: "Are you asking us to deal with a set of outlaws?" And he proceeded to instruct the President in his responsibilities: ". . . I now ask you to perform the duties invested in you as President of the United States, to at once squelch the anarchistic conditions of affairs existing in the anthracite coal regions by the strong arm of the military at your command."

Baer and Markle had threatened the wrong man. Roosevelt kept his temper, but just barely. Inwardly

CULVER SERVICE

NURSERY RHYMES FOR INFANT INDUSTRIES.

Little Boy Blue, come blow your horn;
There are trusts in the meadow and trusts in the corn!
To curb the fat trusts not an effort he'll make,
As a champion sleeper he captures the cake!

*These two cartoons, which appeared in the*
New York Journal *during the strike, are the*

he was seething. Afterward he said, speaking of Baer: "If it wasn't for the high office I hold, I would have taken him by the seat of the breeches and the nape of the neck and chucked him out of that window." And again: "There was only one man in that conference who acted like a gentleman, and that man was not I." The reference was to Mitchell. Indeed, the President wrote to his friend Joseph Bucklin Bishop: "Mitchell shone so in comparison with [the operators] as to make me have a very uncomfortable feeling that they might be far more to blame relatively to the miners than I had supposed. I never knew six men to show to less advantage." That was, in fact, the only effect the meeting had: to convince the President that maybe the miners were right.

Once the conference had failed, however, there seemed little he could do. He had no power to send federal troops, as Markle had demanded, unless the governor of Pennsylvania asked for them. But that

NURSERY RHYMES FOR INFANT INDUSTRIES.

Old King Coal was a jolly old soul,
    And a jolly old soul was he:
When he felt in the humor
He'd rob the consumer
    And chuckle with fiendish glee.

*work of Frederick B. Opper, famous political cartoonist and creator of* Happy Hooligan.

did not for a moment discourage the President. "The one condition Roosevelt's spirit could not endure," his friend Mark Sullivan wrote, "was any situation in which individuals or groups seemed able to defy or ignore the people as a whole and their representative in the White House. . . . He could not endure to be dared." If a request from the governor was necessary, Roosevelt would make sure one came. Through Senator Matthew Quay of Pennsylvania he sought to persuade Stone to ask for federal assistance; then he would send in the Army to operate the mines. He had even chosen a troop commander—Major General J. M. Schofield. But the Quay-Stone gambit failed: no request for troops ever came.

Nevertheless, sentiment for a settlement of some kind continued to build up. The operators were under particularly heavy pressure. Roosevelt was too shrewd a politician not to let some word of his take-over plan get through to them. In addition, their conduct at the Washington conference, coming on top of Baer's infamous letter, placed the coal-hungry public even more squarely behind the miners. The strike had now been in progress for almost five months. Violence was increasing; the entire Pennsylvania National Guard—8,750 strong—was now on duty in the coal region.

To Secretary of War Root, who on his own initiative had carefully reviewed the proceedings of the October 3 meeting, it seemed clear that the strike had now reached the point where pride, more than the issues, prevented either side from backing down. He felt the only hope of settlement lay in an agreement similar to the one Mitchell had suggested: the miners to return to work pending appointment of an impartial board of arbitration whose award both they and the operators would consent in advance to accept.

Still on his own hook, but with Roosevelt's acquiescence, Root on October 11 met with J. P. Morgan in New York. Together they worked out a memorandum —which Morgan next day persuaded Baer and his colleagues to sign—asking Roosevelt to set up an arbitration commission. The operators did not, however, entirely abandon their pride. Though they refrained from naming the members for him, they told the President exactly what kinds of men to select: an engineer from one of the military services, a professional mining engineer, a federal judge from the eastern district of Pennsylvania, a businessman familiar with the anthracite industry, and, finally, "a man of prominence, eminent as a sociologist."

Roosevelt was chagrined—and so was Mitchell, when he learned of the memorandum—to note that not one man with a labor background had been suggested. Both felt there should be at least one such individual,

*The Chicago* Record-Herald *saw George Baer reaching for a large cookie, "Unconditional Surrender" (of the strikers). The public, ordering him to settle for "Arbitration," says: "Hurry up and take the smaller one, Mr. Baer!"*

and that in addition, because so many of the miners were Catholics, a high-ranking Catholic prelate ought to be named. The operators could not very well oppose the latter suggestion, but they could and did fight very vigorously the naming of any pro-labor representative. A crisis was reached late in the evening of October 15. Roosevelt and two of Morgan's junior partners, Bacon and George W. Perkins, were in the White House with telephone lines open to the offices of Morgan and Baer. All at once there ensued a scene of high comedy, which only Roosevelt could appreciate fully; for suddenly it dawned on him "that the mighty brains of these captains of industry would rather have anarchy than tweedledum, but that if I would use the word tweedledee they would hail it as meaning peace." The President explained:

. . . it never occurred to me that the operators were willing to run all this risk on a mere point of foolish pride; but Bacon finally happened to mention that they would not object to any latitude I chose under the headings that they had given. I instantly said that I should appoint my labor man as the "eminent sociologist." To my intense relief, this utter absurdity was received with delight by Bacon and Perkins who said they were sure the operators would agree to it! Morgan and Baer gave their consent by telephone and the thing was done.

To Finley Peter Dunne, creator of Mr. Dooley, Roosevelt wrote: "I feel like throwing up my hands and going to the circus, but as that is not possible I think I shall try a turkey shoot or bear hunt . . ." For the benefit of the country, however, he played it straight: in naming as the "eminent sociologist" E. E. Clark, Grand Chief of the Order of Railway Conductors, the White House spokesman added, with tongue in cheek, ". . . the President assuming that for the purpose of such a commission the term sociologist means a man who has thought and studied deeply on social questions and has practically applied his knowledge."

John Lancaster Spalding, Bishop of Peoria, Illinois, was the Catholic prelate selected, and the other members of the commission were Judge George Gray of the United States Circuit Court, who was elected chairman; Edward W. Parker, editor of the *Engineering and Mining Record;* Thomas H. Watkins, a businessman who for twenty years had operated a mine in Scranton; and Brigadier General John M. Wilson, formerly the Army's Chief of Engineers. "Clark and Spalding," wrote Walter Wellman, "would be set down as leaning toward the miners; Parker and Watkins to the owners; with Gray and Wilson as wholly neutral." The President also appointed Labor Commissioner Wright as recorder, and the others promptly elected him a full member of the commission. Roosevelt had chosen an extremely well-qualified group, and in the process had managed to please both parties to the strike. The miners returned to work and the commission members, after a personal inspection tour of the mines, began their formal hearings in Scranton on November 14. There, in a high-ceilinged Victorian courtroom, economic feudalism went on trial.

No one, apparently, expected that the hearings would be brief, and Judge Gray allowed lawyers for all three factions—the nonunion mine workers were presenting their case separately—as much time as they wished. As a result, the hearings continued, in Scranton and later in Philadelphia, for over three months, with a recess at Christmas. A total of 558 witnesses were heard—240 for the United Mine Workers, 153 for the nonunion men, 154 for the operators, and eleven called by the commission itself. The fifty-six volumes of testimony—by turns bitter and shocking, funny and sad—constitutes a remarkable historical document.

As chief of its legal staff the union had hired Clarence Darrow, who in the next quarter century would make his name as the ablest defense attorney in modern courtroom history. Darrow, playing his cards skillfully, led with his ace: he called John Mitchell to the stand.

If any members of the commission had expected a wild-eyed, fire-eating agitator, they were soon disappointed. Mitchell, dressed as usual in his near-clerical black, the strain of the long strike written clearly in his still-youthful face, stated the union's case calmly and fairly. After Darrow had completed his friendly questioning, Wayne MacVeagh, a former United States attorney general, took over for the operators. His long and grueling cross-examination lasted more than four days, but not once—despite ample provocation—did Mitchell lose his temper. On the contrary, he managed occasionally to enliven the proceedings with rare darts of dry wit. MacVeagh had been badgering him about how, when profits were low, he expected the operators to give the men a raise without passing it on to the consumers, many of whom were poor families:

MACVEAGH: . . . If you demand an increase and they have no profits, where are they going to place it except on the bowed backs of the poor?

MITCHELL: They might put it on the bowed backs of the rich.

With one eye on the commission, the other on public opinion, Darrow followed Mitchell with 239 witnesses, for the most part ordinary miners and their families. Day after day, week after week, there moved across the stand a pitiable parade of the blinded and maimed, the widowed and orphaned, the oppressed and exploited. Darrow was also careful to include a generous leavening of priests and ministers—and in truth such men were in the majority among the minefield clergy—who favored the union's cause. Compared with their powerful stories, the testimony of the nonunion miners and that of the operators' witnesses fails to move one nearly so deeply, at least when read at a remove of nearly sixty years.

But the hearings did more than lengthen the short and simple annals of the poor. The last two men the commission heard before adjourning to consider its decision were Baer, summing up for the operators, and Darrow, for the miners. American history rarely presents such an opportunity to study within a narrow compass the contrast between two utterly opposed philosophies of the social order. Baer—spade-bearded, almond-eyed, self-assured, quoting Seneca, Cervantes, and the Roman law—spoke for the glories of the half century just passed, when capitalism was unrestricted and capitalists answered only to their stockholders. Darrow—given to the florid phrase and the dramatic gesture—spoke for the century just beginning, which would assert the rights of the individual workingman and his union, and would bring an end to the world George Baer had known. A few statements from their long summations, selected at random and juxtaposed, will point up the contrast:

BAER: . . . we do not admit the right of an organization . . . to coerce us . . . or [interfere] with our management. The employer ought, I think, to meet his employees personally . . .

DARROW: . . . these gentlemen who all these long and weary months have refused to know us, to recognize us, have demanded as a condition that these men must give up their union . . . and must come to them with their hat in their hand, each one in a position to be discharged the next moment if they dare to raise their voice.

BAER: [The strike furnished] a record of lawlessness and crimes unparalleled in any community save where contending armies met on fields of legal battle . . .

DARROW: So far as the demands of the Mine Workers are concerned, it makes no difference whether crimes have been committed or not. If John Smith earned $500 a year, it is no answer to say that Tom Jones murdered somebody in cold blood. . . . The question is, what has [Smith] earned?

BAER: If a man comes to me and offers to work for me and I am willing to pay him $2 a day and he is content to take it, that is a bargain as good and as sacred in the eyes of the law as any bargain could be . . .

DARROW: Mr. Baer and his friends imagine no doubt that they are fighting for a grand principle when they fight for what they say is the God-given right of every man to work for any wages he sees fit. . . . But that is not [the] God-given right these gentlemen are interested in. They are interested in the God-given right to hire the cheapest man they can get.

BAER: . . . the eight-hour system, it is proposed, shall bring about . . . the leisure to enable [the miners] to

**DUMPED RIGHT IN THE WAY.**

*Stubbornness of the "Coal Trust" blocked prosperity, the* Ohio State Journal *believed.*

learn to read good novels and sound religious books. (Laughter)

DARROW: It is no answer to say, as some employers have said in this case, "If you give him shorter hours he will not use them wisely." . . . One man may stumble; ten men may stumble; but in the long sweep of time, and in the evolution of events, it must be that greater opportunities mean a more perfect man . . .

And Darrow had the last word:

The blunders are theirs, and the victories have been ours. The blunders are theirs because, [in] this old, old strife they are fighting for slavery, while we are fighting for freedom. They are fighting for the rule of man over man, for despotism, for darkness, for the past. We are striving to build up man. We are working for democracy, for humanity, for the future, for the days that will come too late for us to see it or know it or receive its benefits, but which still will come . . .

And so it has turned out.

When the commission finally announced its award on March 22, 1903, it granted the contract miners a ten per cent wage increase, and there were a few other gains important enough for the rank and file of the strikers to regard the settlement as a victory. Yet since the primary object of the strike—recognition of the United Mine Workers—was not achieved, there were those who said that the miners had lost the strike. But what mattered more was that they had won the battle of public opinion; formal recognition of their union would come. And quite as important—for organized labor and for the nation as a whole—the federal government, for the first time in its history, had intervened in a strike not to break it, but to bring about a peaceful settlement. The great anthracite strike of 1902 cast a long shadow.

Roosevelt went to Mississippi for his bear hunt, and Lodge and the Republicans got their majority at the polls. For Mitchell, however, the fruits of victory were bitter. He stayed on as the United Mine Workers president for five more years, but they were years full of factionalism and eventually, in 1907, he failed to win re-election. The opposition, it was true, came mostly from the bituminous delegates; in the anthracite John Mitchell was still a demigod. But the defeat was final, for all that.

Mitchell was still a young man, but there seemed nothing for him to do. There was some talk of his succeeding Samuel Gompers as president of the American Federation of Labor, and later of his becoming the first Secretary of Labor when Woodrow Wilson made that appointment in 1913. But neither job materialized. Away from the union and the mines Mitchell was lost, and he died, frustrated and worn out, in 1919. He was forty-nine.

# The Moving Image

CONTINUED FROM PAGE 34

mon could not hold their monopoly, Porter met a fellow adventurer, an itinerant medicine man who had been cleaning up in the Caribbean on Indian Miracle Oil. They bought an interest in the International Projectorscope, an imitation of the Vitascope, and the rights for the West Indies. Porter had graduated from projectionist to promoter, and set sail for Jamaica and Costa Rica to make his fortune. Years later he confessed to Terry Ramsaye, the screen's first historian, that he billed himself there as "Mr. Thomas A. Edison, Jr.," his nom de plume "for use in foreign parts only." Filmdom was a lawless frontier in those days.

Adventures followed one upon the other. Porter went to work for Kuhn and Webster, projecting the first advertising films on a billboard facing Herald Square, from a booth on top of the Pepper Building. Crowds jammed the streets; Porter was arrested on a charge of blocking traffic. Next, he toured Quebec and Nova Scotia with the Projectorscope, accompanying the renowned Wormwood's Dog and Monkey Show. Then he went to work for Eden Musée, the most illustrious exhibition hall in the land, which sponsored a film version of the celebrated Passion play in twenty-four scenes, alleged to have been photographed at Oberammergau. As it happened, the camels, donkeys, and actors had gone through their paces on the roof of the Grand Central Palace in New York. Porter was getting his apprenticeship in the film business.

By this time Edison was starting suits for patent infringement, and Porter shrewdly decided to go to work for the Wizard as a cameraman. An early assignment was to photograph Sir Thomas Lipton's famous sailboat *Shamrock I*, and he succeeded beautifully, catching her with her sails against the sun, her hull gliding through the sparkling sea. Edison had reduced the size and weight of the Kinetograph, so that the camera could take to the open road, shooting fire engines, horse and car traffic, trains pounding around curves, as well as set pieces inside Black Maria. Recorded (or subject) movement had been augmented by manipulated (or camera) movement. Promio, a cameraman of Louis Lumière of France, had shot the

Grand Canal of Venice from a gondola in 1896; that same year Dickson, who had left Edison for the Biograph Company, had shot a *Panorama of the American and Canadian Falls*. What hadn't as yet been accomplished was mounted, or edited, movement. This was to be Porter's unique contribution, and it earned him the title of "father of the story film."

To appreciate Porter's revolutionary approach, one might compare his work with productions of the same period in France and England. In the fall of 1894 Edison had exported several Kinetoscopes to help him realize part of his investment—a most curious move, inasmuch as the Wizard had neglected to protect himself with an international patent. Two enterprising Greeks, George Georgiades and George Trajedis, who had been greengrocers in England, returned to London with Kinetoscopes purchased from Edison's eastern agents. One Lionel Werner did the same, and opened a Kinetoscope parlor in Paris at 20 Boulevard Poissonnière in October, 1894. In a letter to Terry Ramsaye, Louis and Auguste Lumière, photographic manufacturers in Lyons, admitted that they got into the business when they strolled down the Champs-Élysées one day, spied a Kinetoscope in a shop, and promptly bought it.

The master magician of the Lumière camera was Georges Méliès, a theatrical prestidigitator who discovered that camera tricks could be achieved by manipulating the crank—for example: reverse motion, slow motion, superimposition (double exposure), fade-ins and fade-outs. However, the trick shot in *The Execution of Mary Queen of Scots* by Heise preceded by at least a year Méliès' accidental discovery of stop-motion when his camera jammed. In his country place in Montreuil, Méliès built a studio stage equipped with trap doors, overhead pulleys, and machines to produce sea waves, wind, and clouds. Méliès proudly claimed, and rightly so, that he was the first to "push the cinema toward the theatrical way." But for all his fertile imagination and audacity, his shots remained stage tableaux.

Porter was impressed by the number of sets Méliès employed to tell a tale of magical adventure, as he had been impressed by the twenty-four scenes in the Passion play, but he was unimpressed by the rigid perspective, as of a spectator seated in the orchestra. Porter found what he was looking for in the work of the British photographers, James Williamson and G. A. Smith of Brighton, who used cameras manufactured by Robert William Paul of London. In 1899 Williamson took six shots of a Royal Henley Regatta, from the beginning to the end of the race. The remarkable feature in what might otherwise have been

*The "Searchlight" Theater in Tacoma, Washington, one of the first to show Edison's motion pictures in the Northwest, printed this bill at the turn of the century.*

an ordinary news film was Williamson's use of inserted shots, taken from a boat, of the crowd cheering on shore. This seems to have been the very first expression of the camera's power, through cutting and splicing the film, to give an audience two points of view concurrently: in this instance, the race as seen

101

from the shore, the crowd as observed from a boat.

In December, 1901, Williamson produced an enacted newsreel, *Fire!,* in which a man was rescued from a burning building. It was undramatic, but Porter, remembering some news shots he had made of fire engines, decided to edit these and add others to tell a story. In doing so he added plot to reality, and it was like adding life to facts.

That Porter's impetus came from Williamson's *Fire!,* imported by the rival Biograph Company, shows how early the stage adage—"one hit deserves another" —was practiced by the new industry. Nothing was sacred. Williamson faked the Boer War and Boxer Rebellion in his backyard garden; the Spanish-American War was enacted in the Jersey hills, and so on. But Porter's *Life of an American Fireman* (June, 1903) was not only Edison's answer to Biograph's *Fire!* It was the first drama to be photographed free from stage perspective. Porter released movies from their theatrical picture frame. His simple story of a

*Silhouettes of Leland Stanford's horse "Sallie Gardner," photographed in motion by Muybridge, Palo Alto, June 19, 1878.*

fire chief, the trapped wife and child, and their rescue was primitive but genuine art.

Porter became the first in the new art to let content determine form. Thus, with the fire engines arriving before the burning building, a fireman hopping off with hose in hand, Porter makes us feel the excitement by pivoting his camera with the action from the road to the house. This is probably the first dramatic-narrative panoramic shot in history. At its very climax, Porter tilts his camera upward to reveal the mother in her nightgown waving in an upstairs window. Also, his use of the close-up (the fire box), though not new, has a dynamic effect of narrative surprise.

In this early masterpiece of twenty-six shots (Pathé version) Porter directs our attention to the action as he wishes to describe it. Starting with a shot in which the mother jumps out of bed and amid thick smoke rushes to the window, he begins to alternate interior and exterior shots in perfect counterpoint and in faster tempo until his climax. Some are mere flashes on the screen—a little over two feet of film—the mother frantic on the street, the fireman in the burning room reaching for the baby. Two decades later, Eisenstein

and Pudovkin, the renowned Russian director-editors, won international acclaim for refining what Porter had inaugurated. *Fireman* has a rightful claim to be considered the single most important film in the history of the Moving Image.

Porter's next revolutionary step was the juggling of narrative time. The trapped mother and child and the ride to the rescue in *Fireman* had suggested parallel action. What Porter now did in his second masterpiece, *The Great Train Robbery,* shot in the fall of the same year, was to relate parallel action with shifts in time. He had undoubtedly seen an English film, produced in May or June of 1903, called *Robbery of a Mail Coach,* which also had parallel story development. But in his new film Porter juggled time by having scenes start before previous scenes had ended, such as the cowboys dancing in the saloon, who are then interrupted by the arrival of the railroad clerk, the latter freed by his daughter from the bandits' gag and ropes during an earlier shot.

Porter saved the film medium from being an extension of the stage. He went on to do social-content films, *The Ex-Convict* and *The Kleptomaniac,* and to outdo Méliès in fantasy with *The Dream of a Rarebit Fiend.* He founded his own company, Rex, and joined with Adolph Zukor in the Famous Players Company. He directed Pauline Frederick, John Barrymore, and Mary Pickford (in *Tess of the Storm Country,* which grossed a million dollars from a $13,000 budget—the best record in the business). But it is for *The Life of an American Fireman* and *The Great Train Robbery* that his fame is most secure. He was the first creative artist of the Moving Image. At forty-three he retired with his fortune, then lost it in the crash of 1929. He lived out his years in the Hotel Taft, near Broadway, virtually unknown and shamefully unhonored.

At this point, the motion picture having become independent as an art, it might appear that there were no new or basic contributions to be made. But Porter can be said to have charted only the iceberg above the surface. D. W. Griffith discovered how vast a bulk lay below.

Toward the end of 1907 Griffith, a young playwright from Kentucky who had already toured on the road and suffered his first flop, rode the Third Avenue "El" to the Edison studio in the Bronx. He offered Porter a script based on the opera *Tosca,* but Porter thought it too pretentious. Instead of a sale, the hungry author got an acting role. He was thirty-two.

All his life David Wark Griffith—a tall, lean man with an arresting face—remained in love with the theater. During his early successes at the Biograph studios in New York he confided to his wife, the stage actress Linda Arvidson, "They [motion pictures] can't last, I give them a few years. . . . Nobody's going to know I ever did this sort of thing when I'm a famous playwright." In his twenty-three-year career he made 484 films, spent over twenty million dollars and earned sixty million. He died dodging lawsuits (he was actually unable to appear publicly in New York City), having made no pictures at all during the last seventeen years of his life. He was a man disappointed, but unbowed: shortly before his death in Hollywood on July 23, 1948, I lunched with this proud, lonely personage, and he had a play script under his arm!

He was to elaborate on this technique throughout his career, so much so that his name became associated with short, rapid editing in an exciting style, leading to a last-minute rescue. Griffith was called a "dangerous influence" by a number of critics simply because, as an artist, he evoked the passions of audiences to a degree previously unknown. He did so primarily by taking his intimate shots and editing them, not only in the narrative progression of Porter, but also for their emotional, descriptive, and ideological values.

Griffith's first editing for emotion appears to have been his adaptation of Tennyson's *Enoch Arden,* called *After Many Years* (October, 1908). To show Annie Lee lonely, as she waits for her husband's appearance, he moved the camera from an establishing shot of Annie Lee to a close-up of her brooding face. But how could anyone tell what she was brooding about? So the third shot showed the subject of her concern, her husband cast away on a desert island.

During the next year the poet in Griffith came for-

CULVER SERVICE

The irony of Griffith is that in bringing the Moving Image to the form it is in today, he relegated his true love, the theater, to the status of a less popular art. Griffith never valued his eminent position as first master of the art of motion pictures. His typical remark after a projection-room screening was, "Well, it's a helluva way to earn a living."

What was the essence of Griffith's genius? His contribution came precisely from being a poet (frustrated in print) who saw in terms of images, and an actor (frustrated on the boards) who made the camera a participant. His improvements on the work of Porter and others, and his own innovations or rediscoveries, sprang from this double advantage.

A stage director is oriented to the audience, but an actor is oriented to his fellow actors. Griffith's viewpoint tended to be, whenever possible, in the midst of the action. He first broke with stage direction while directing *For Love of Gold,* which he adapted in 1908 from Jack London's *Just Meat.* In a scene in which two men seated at a table become distrustful of each other, Griffith asked himself, "How can I show what they are thinking?" His answer: Bring the camera closer to the actors. So, figuratively speaking, he took the audience from their seats and moved them onto the stage. This had been done before, but not—as Griffith did it—in the very middle of a scene.

ward, and he added descriptive editing—the cutting from one shot to another purely for visual or aesthetic effect. In *Edgar Allan Poe,* produced in January, 1909, and based on *The Raven,* he used light and shade, a klieg light striking the brow of Poe as he declaimed. In that film Henry "Walt" Walthall, later to become famous as the Little Colonel in *The Birth of a Nation,* recited a line from "To One In Paradise"—"And all my days are trances." All his days, Griffith had an affinity for Poe. His own poems, nakedly sentimental, make his title inserts embarrassing to read, and explain in part why he failed to keep abreast of post-World War I sophistication.

Lighting to convey mood was further advanced in *The Drunkard's Reformation* (March, 1909), when Griffith illuminated his actors' faces by the glow of firelight from simulated flames. The cameramen, Bitzer and Marvin, protested: the players would scarcely be seen in the flickering shadows; but Griffith had a proud and vocal disdain for obstacles. Controlled lighting was extended to narrative as well as description in *Pippa Passes* (October, 1909, adapted from Browning): the sun's first rays awaken Pippa as she sleeps; then soft lights usher in the morning, and full, the bright day. In his later work Griffith often employed descriptive editing to indicate the setting—

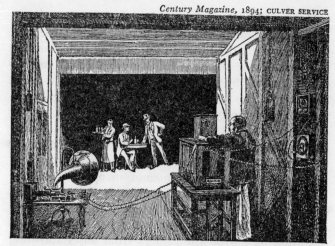

*The interior of Edison's studio, the "Black Maria," so-called for its exterior resemblance to a police wagon.*

the carefully composed long shots lend atmosphere in *Ramona* (May, 1910); and to depict characters—in *Intolerance* (1916) he juxtaposed people with symbolic birds: the close-up of a pair of doves drawing a toy chariot and its flowers between Belshazzar and the Princess Beloved, the close-ups of Dear One and baby chicks, of Jesus and the doves, and so on.

By the time Griffith took his company of Biograph players to California in the winter of 1910, he had explored enough of the new medium to realize that movies had left the stage far behind. Out of his own need to fulfill himself as an artist, Griffith expanded and refined the camera innovations of others, giving them his individual trademark. His predecessor at the Biograph studio, Wallace McCutchen, had photographed a chase from an automobile, and even earlier, in 1903, Alfred Collins of British Gaumont had used shots from moving cars. Griffith did it more masterfully and more dramatically. At the Sunset Boulevard studio the sun hardly set without at least one camera on wheels—the trucking-shot technique that Griffith used to perfection in *The Birth of a Nation*, when the Klans ride to their various rescues.

By taking one final step forward, Griffith brought the motion-picture art to maturity. He added touches of editorial comment or symbolism for social or political emphasis, a technique subsequently imitated by Eisenstein and Pudovkin. His two greatest masterpieces, *The Birth of a Nation* and *Intolerance*, bristle with such juxtapositions of argument and plot, fact and fiction. Both films carry the quality of epics because their creator had a burning passion to rewrite history in his own image. In *Intolerance*, Christ, Belshazzar (Babylon's betrayed king), the massacred Huguenots, and Modern Man (victimized by strikes, poverty, crime, charity, and the courts)—all are portrayed as sacrifices to "despotism and injustice." The four historical stories unfold first separately and then together, linked by Griffith's ideological editing. It is a picture ahead of its time, and our time.

Within an eight-year period (1908-16) Griffith brought the Moving Image to its peak, and today we are coasting on his achievement. Looking back, it is clear that Edison regarded the Kinetoscope and Kinetograph as machines for novel entertainment; Porter considered the craft unique as a storyteller and a money-maker; and Griffith became the master of an art form he unwittingly brought to maturity. Since then, sound and color have arrived, and the television camera and receiver—also perfected near the Hudson River—have added long-distance transmission to the medium's capabilities. When the future passes judgment on this era, it will not be surprising if the art of the Moving Image ranks high among our creative accomplishments.

---

*Robert Gessner, professor of motion pictures at New York University, has also been a screen writer, novelist, and poet. He is president of the newly organized Society of Cinematologists, devoted to the study of film as an art.*

★ ★ ★ ★ ★ ★ ★ ★ ★ ★ ★ ★ ★ ★ ★ ★ ★ ★ ★ ★ ★ ★ ★

## SHREWDNESS AT THE SUMMIT, *or,* WHO OUTFOXED WHOM?

American bumptiousness has always been offensive but the abasement that goes with it is worse, for it has been deceptive. . . . the most serious mistake of Europe has always been to misunderstand [the Americans'] romanticism, which is the consequence of having lived a Cinderella story. It has been repeatedly mistaken for softness, gullibility, decadence. Their smile is childlike and bland; they affect an innocence and credulity which the European mind has accepted as real. Yet from Franklin and John Jay on, their negotiators have usually come back not only with all that the adept cynicism of their opponents undertook to take from them by means of a cold deck, but with the scarf pins, cuff links, and pocket watches of the cynical as well. For the romanticism is the thinnest possible veneer. There have been no such realists since the Romans and they are the hardest empiricists of the modern world.

*Bernard DeVoto, in the centennial issue of* Harper's Magazine, *reprinted in* The Easy Chair, *Houghton Mifflin, 1955.*

# One-shot War with England CONTINUED FROM PAGE 64

Charles Griffin, owner of the pig, and Lyman A. Cutler, who shot the beast.

In his report to Governor Douglas, Griffin, who was the company agent on San Juan, hotly and somewhat incoherently described "an outrage committed here today by a man by the name of Cutler, an American, who has very recently established himself on a prairie occupied by me and close to my establishment, he has dug up about one third of an acre in which he planted potatoes and partly and very imperfectly enclosed, my cattle & pigs had free access to the patch."

Griffin then went on to relate with equal emphasis how his valuable pig had been wantonly slain while peacefully rooting some distance from Cutler's potatoes. Subsequently, Cutler had appeared at Griffin's door and offered "remuneration which was so insignificant it only added insult to injury, and likewise used the most insulting & threatening language."

Cutler, with comparable reluctance to bring a sentence to an end, saw the incident somewhat differently:

For some time passed I have been greatly anoyed by one of the Hudson Bay Co. hogs (black Boar) entering my potatoe patch and destroying the crop, he was repeatedly driven off by myself back to the Hudson Bay Co (a distance of one and a half mile) and the Hudson Bay Co was aware of this fact. In the morning of the 15th Inst I was aroused by some person riding by on horseback and upon going out the door found it to be Jacob, a colard man one of the Hudson Bay Co servants, I immediately glanced toward the potatoe patch (which is directly along side the road) and seen the Hudson Bay Co hog at his old game. I immediately became enraged at the independance of the negro knowing as he did my previous loss and upon the impulse of the moment seazed my rifle and shot the hog.

Far from using "the most insulting & threatening language," Cutler stated in his affidavit, he had then proceeded to Griffin's house eager to apologize for his burst of temper, only to be met by "supercilious manners," a threat of arrest, and a demand for a staggering one hundred dollars in damages, which he flatly rejected.

The following day the British warship *Satellite* hove into view, carrying to San Juan a special envoy with orders to bring Cutler to Victoria for trial. Cutler, still fuming, refused to surrender. Flourishing his rifle, he made it plain that he would blow the emissary's head off rather than submit to arrest.

The commanding general of United States forces in the area at this time was Brigadier General W. S. Harney; his headquarters were at the former Hudson's Bay Company post, Fort Vancouver. Harney, who ap-

pears to have had all the instincts of a fire horse, was already darkly suspicious of British motives in respect to San Juan Island. The presence of three ships of war in the nearby waters made him uneasy, and he accepted at face value the rumors that the English were plotting to unleash a horde of hostile Indians against the American settlers.

Harney was convinced that San Juan was an outpost of major strategic importance, not to be given up under any circumstances. In his view, the bay on the southeastern shore of the island was the best location for a naval base on the entire Pacific Coast. He was also aware of the difficulty that the English had encountered in their efforts to promote colonization of their holdings in British Columbia. With the promise of ten acres of land, the Hudson's Bay Company had induced many families to migrate from the barren Orkney Islands north of Scotland. Through the grapevine, however, these settlers quickly learned that less than a day's journey distant, the United States was giving away 640-acre parcels, and many realists among them coolly picked up and moved to take advantage of the better deal.

This led General Harney to include in his reports to the War Department the observation that the British were unable to colonize their holdings, being "too exacting," and to propose that Vancouver Island, as well as San Juan, might properly be part of the U.S.

When he learned of the attempted arrest of Lyman

*Brigadier General William S. Harney, a violent Anglophobe, sent Pickett to occupy the disputed territory.*

Cutler, Harney went into a frenzy of activity to counter what he regarded as an act of aggression, as well as to remove further question as to the rightful ownership of San Juan Island and to establish a bridgehead for any future operations that might be authorized.

The U.S. Army unit nearest San Juan was Company D, 9th Infantry, stationed at Bellingham under the command of Captain George E. Pickett, who later won immortality as a Confederate general at Gettysburg. Harney ordered Pickett to San Juan without delay, alerted the rest of his command to move to Pickett's aid, and called on the Navy to "send such force as you can render available."

On July 27, Pickett landed on San Juan with his fifty men and pitched camp near the southeast tip of the island. He had two primary missions: to protect the inhabitants against further "outrages" by the British and to warn off the Indians. "Should these Indians appear peaceable," he was told by Harney, "you will warn them in a quiet but firm manner to return to their own country; and in the event of any opposition being offered to your demands, you will use the most decisive methods to enforce them."

As it turned out, the Indians steered clear of the excitement, and Captain Pickett's full attention was reserved for the British. Their first move came in the form of a written communication from Charles Griffin—who, as a justice of the peace, was the resident authority—notifying the troops that they were on Hudson's Bay Company property and pointedly inviting them to depart. Pickett reported "tremendous" excitement around his campsite. An estimated five hundred persons came to see the soldiers, and several who had brought their weapons with them volunteered as reinforcements.

Communications of warning, remonstrance, and protest were at this point flying back and forth at all levels of authority. But Governor Douglas' past experience told him that he would be foolish to rely on the professional diplomats for a quick and satisfactory solution. He resolved to dislodge Pickett—if this was feasible—and to preserve the *status quo* if it was not. Douglas reasoned that the bigger the American forces on San Juan and the longer they were dug in, the harder it would be to drive them back to the continent.

CULVER SERVICE

*Captain George Pickett, later a Confederate general, led the U.S. companies at San Juan Island.*

Sending the H.M.S. *Tribune* on reconnaissance, the Governor soon learned that Pickett's men were so disposed that it would require a sizable force to round them up in an orderly fashion. The Americans held a piece of ground flanked by heavy scrub growth into which they might easily scatter. Ruling out direct action against Pickett, Douglas attempted instead to prevent reinforcements from reaching him.

A succession of parleys ensued. Governor Douglas' various representatives sought to impress Pickett that he should withdraw, but Pickett stood on his orders to remain. On August 3, after a polite but disquieting conference with the captains of all three British warships, the American commander rejected a proposal for a joint military occupation, and sent a plea for reinforcements. Receiving Pickett's message, Harney ordered five companies waiting on the mainland to charter the necessary steamers and move to San Juan Island, taking all field guns and every bit of ammunition they could muster.

By mid-August, the U.S. force on the island had swelled to nine companies, backed by eight 32-pounders. At the northern end of the island were arrayed 2,140 redcoats, including 600 Royal Marines and engineer troops, supported by five warships and 167 guns.

Meanwhile in Washington, Lord Lyons, the British minister, haunted the State Department, pleading for information. But Secretary Lewis Cass offered him only slight comfort by expressing the "regret of the President at the recent difficulties" and the hope that no serious consequences would result.

There were some who later suspected Harney, Pickett, and other pro-Southern Democrats in the Washington Territory of deliberately seeking to draw England into open conflict, with the hope of diverting their fellow Americans from the issues that threatened to provoke civil strife between North and South, and thus of helping to save the Union. According to General George B. McClellan, who served as a member of an army survey mission to the Territory in the late 1850's, the Harney-Pickett element was ready to fight the British if that could avert disunion. In the years after the Civil War, McClellan and Pickett's widow circulated this story widely. If, however, any such conspiracy existed, the plotters left no documentary traces.

Washington finally decided that a firm hand was needed at San Juan. The Chief of Staff of the Army, seventy-three-year-old Lieutenant General Winfield Scott, was picked to dash across the continent and exert a calming influence. There was always the chance, of course, that Scott, upon his arrival, would find the opposing forces locked in combat. If such was the case, he should not "suffer the national honor to be tarnished. If we must be forced into a war by the violence of the British authorities, which is not anticipated, we shall abide the issue as best we may without apprehension as to the result."

Fortunately, when the elderly peacemaker arrived he found the antagonists still merely glaring at one another. Giving the order to stand fast, he quickly got in touch with Governor Douglas for the purpose of arranging a withdrawal of the bulk of the troops.

Agreement did not come easily. Douglas strenuously opposed continued occupation by a single U.S. soldier, while Scott came under pressure from San Juan's American civilians to provide a guard adequate to repel marauding Indians. Douglas, after extended negotiation, agreed to the presence of a token force.

Meanwhile, General Harney was rebuked for his hotheadedness. He was relieved and sent back to Washington.

Came the Civil War and whatever happened on San Juan Island during that period went unrecorded. The "temporary" occupation by the small detachment of U.S. troops was maintained, however, and after Appomattox the impasse persisted, once more to plague the diplomats.

Actually the British-American ownership dispute was not alone responsible for the final solution of the San Juan problem. It seemed that the American civilian authorities and the military on the island had become engaged in an acrimonious conflict over who had paramount jurisdiction. Tension reached a climax when a resentful farmer stretched a wire fence across the road leading from the army camp to the landing. The captain in command promptly ejected the man from the island, whereupon the U.S. district court ordered the captain's arrest.

Warned by the U.S. marshal that trouble was in store unless the issue was quickly resolved, the federal government sent word that the Army should continue to be the dominant authority, lest the territorial claim against Britain be prejudiced.

This failed to cool things off. Repudiating the longstanding arrangements made by General Scott, the government of Washington Territory assumed all fiscal and judicial powers, managed to arrest an army major, and levied a staggering $5,000 fine against the offending captain. Alarmed by these developments, the Department of State hastily obtained British agreement to lay the boundary dispute before the President of Switzerland for arbitration.

But the time was not yet opportune for a compromise. In the years following the Civil War, Northern tempers still raged over the depredations of the British-

*At seventy-three, Winfield Scott, Chief of Staff of the U.S. Army, crossed the continent to settle the San Juan question.*

built Confederate raider *Alabama*. Anglophobic members of Congress not only demanded huge indemnities in payment for the *Alabama* claims, but the surrender of all British Columbia as well. The British reacted by backing away from the boundary negotiations with great rapidity.

By 1871, however, the atmosphere seemed ripe for another try. As British and American diplomats came together to settle the *Alabama* claims and other outstanding matters, the dog-eared problem of the San Juan boundary was quietly handed to Kaiser Wilhelm I of Germany to arbitrate.

On October 21, 1872, "Authenticated by our autographic signature and the impression of the imperial great seal," the Kaiser's decision, based on a fat volume of documentary evidence, placed the final border to the west of San Juan, upholding the United States claim.

The American minister in Berlin, George Bancroft, sent a memorandum to Von Balan, the Kaiser's foreign minister, applauding the end of Anglo-American friction. "After an unrelenting strife of ninety years, the award of His Majesty the Emperor of Germany closes the long and unintermitted, and often very dangerous, series of disputes on the extent of their respective territories, and so for the first time in their histories opens to the two countries the unobstructed way to agreement, good understanding and peace."

*Warren Grant Magnuson, the senior senator from Washington, has served in the upper house since 1944. He joins his colleague from the Pacific Northwest, Richard L. Neuberger, as an* AMERICAN HERITAGE *senatorial author.*

# READING, WRITING, AND HISTORY

*By* BRUCE CATTON

## In Defense of Slavery

One century ago there were plenty of Americans who spoke and wrote in defense of the institution of human slavery. There was a wealth of literature designed to prove not merely that slavery was a necessary evil which could be eradicated only at the cost of a social and economic convulsion, but that it was a positive good, a proper way to get the world's work done. To a comparatively large proportion of Americans this argument seemed logical and convincing.

Then came the Civil War, and slavery went out of existence. It died for a number of reasons, one of them apparently being that it was the one human institution on earth that could not be defended by force of arms, a bigger one perhaps lying in the fact that it simply could not be an enduring foundation for what, after all, was by its origins and its traditions a free society. When slavery died, the attempts to justify it died. American society followed a new line of development, and the impassioned, laboriously reasoned literature which had grown up in slavery's defense became meaningless.

But the course the world has followed in the past century has not quite been the one that seemed inevitable in the unquiet and exhausted dawn that followed Appomattox. Then the individual man's right to be complete master of his own fate looked like a thing guaranteed forever. It was not possible to see that within one hundred years there would be slave societies of a new kind, as coercive and restrictive as anything the cotton belt ever knew, taking on an air of permanence and engendering their own abundant literature of justification.

Of all the Americans who spoke in defense of slavery, one man, perhaps, did have a notion of what might lie ahead. George Fitzhugh, of Caroline, Virginia, has been pronounced "the most logical reactionary in the South," and he thought his way more deeply into the origins and meanings of slavery than any of its other advocates. He embodied his thoughts in a bristling book entitled *Cannibals All!,* and this book, with an excellent introduction by C. Vann Woodward, has just been reissued in the Harvard University Press's John Harvard Library series.

What made Fitzhugh different was that he argued from a different base. Other defenders of the institu-

---

**Cannibals All!** or, Slaves without Masters, by George Fitzhugh, edited by C. Vann Woodward. The Harvard University Press. 320 pp. $4.25.

---

tion were at least, fundamentally, believers in a free society, heirs to the libertarian tradition to which all Americans subscribed. Fitzhugh said flatly that "the unrestricted exploitation of so-called free society is more oppressive to the laborer than domestic slavery." Wage slavery he considered worse than chattel slavery, the idea of human progress he believed to be a delusion, and laissez-faire capitalism struck him as an unmitigated evil. The experiment in liberty and equality, so hopefully undertaken in America and in France, he believed a flat failure. Society, he asserted, was "marching to the utter abandonment of the most essential institutions—religion, family ties, property and the restraints of justice."

Fitzhugh, in short, approved of practically nothing that had happened in the world in the past two centuries. John Locke and the Enlightenment, the whole development of libertarian thought and principles on which all American public men, both North and South, took their stand—all of this, to Fitzhugh, was wrong, productive of evil rather than good. England's "Glorious Revolution" he held a tragic mistake; throne, church, and nobility had lost their power, the House of Commons represented only land and money, and under its despotic rule "the masses have become outlaws." Free society, in Fitzhugh's eyes, exploited its laborers more cruelly than slave society: "It exacts more of its slaves, and neither protects nor governs them."

To buttress his case, Fitzhugh turned to the wealth of material then available on miserable working and living conditions that the early industrial revolution was inflicting on the English proletariat. He used, as a matter of fact, a great deal of the same material Karl Marx was using, indicting capitalism in much the same way Marx indicted it, asserting that exploitation of the worker was the inevitable result of free capitalism: "It is to the interest of the capitalist and the skillful to allow free laborers the least possible portion of the fruits of their own labor; for all capital is created by labor, and the smaller the allowance of the free laborer, the greater the gains of his employer. To treat free laborers badly and unfairly, is universally inculcated as a moral duty, and the selfishness of man's nature prompts him to the most rigorous performance of this cannibalish duty."

Indeed, Fitzhugh asserted that slavery was a form of communism, the slave having a vested right to all of the necessities of life; so, "as the Abolitionists and Socialists have resolved to adopt a new social system, we recommend it to their consideration." White wage earners in the North, he argued, would be better off if formally enslaved as southern Negroes were enslaved: "They would work no harder than they do now . . . would be relieved of most of the cares of life, and let into the enjoyment of all valuable and necessary rights." As to the price these laborers would have to pay he had a contemptuous answer: "What would they lose in liberty and equality? Just nothing."

All of this, to be sure, is an oddity out of the dim past, a bristling and readable polemic in a long-deserted forum; and yet, the world being what it is today, Fitzhugh's argument has a disturbing, haunting quality that goes with no other pre-Civil War defense

of slavery. A good part of the world today is ruled by a creed to which the Fitzhugh thesis would fit with very little readjustment. For millions upon millions of people, the turn to organized slavery has been made to seem like a welcome attainment of security, with the resultant loss in liberty and equality looking like "just nothing." Fitzhugh himself would doubtless be horrified at the result, but if he was an eccentric prophet, he is not, at this date, entirely a dishonored one. As Mr. Woodward points out in his introduction: "Even in those societies where socialism is abhorred, mass production, mass organization and mass culture render his insights more meaningful than they ever were in the old order of individualism." Of all the voices that were raised in defense of chattel slavery, Fitzhugh's is the only one that still has a grim meaning.

## A Voice in Rebuttal

This is not to say that the inverted world which Fitzhugh dimly envisioned is necessarily any more permanent than the slave-based society of the 1850's was, or that the destruction of American chattel slavery was no more than an illusory advance. It does perhaps mean, however, that the values that were involved in the effort to end slavery are still worth re-examination, and that that entire chapter in American history continues to merit study. If freedom is under attack in so many parts of the world today, an intimate look at some of the things that happen when freedom does not exist at all can be valuable.

Testimony on this matter is available from Fitzhugh's own era: a reprint (again in the John Harvard Library series) of the once-famous *Narrative of the Life of Frederick Douglass, an American Slave, Written by Himself,* presented now in an edition edited by Benjamin Quarles. Douglass' narrative makes a good companion piece for *Cannibals All!* The benefits of slavery, so eloquently upheld by Fitzhugh, seem totally invisible in this account written by a man who had himself been a slave.

Douglass wrote this book when the heat was still on. He escaped from slavery in 1838 and wrote his book in 1845, and there was at that time a fairly good chance that he might be seized and carried back into bondage; and in the days when he hammered the thing out, no one could say with any confidence that the institution of human slavery would not go on and on into the indefinite future. It was literally dangerous, when he wrote, for any man to say that he had given Frederick Douglass help; it was even more dangerous for Douglass himself to tell where he had come from and what had happened to him; and, all in all, here is a word coming out of the blackest pit, written at a time when freedom was a magic word and liberty was perhaps nothing better than a flickering marsh fire that would die unless someone was prepared to die for it.

Douglass did not know much about himself. Rather vaguely, he was aware that he had been born somewhere around 1817; he had seen his mother "to know her as such" no more than four or five times in his life, usually very briefly and at night, and he grew up knowing nothing better than the life of the stalled ox or the mule, a wholly owned creature with no rights that anyone was bound to respect. He did not come from the Deep South. Oddly enough, this man who wrote one of the most damning indictments of slavery was held in servitude in Maryland, where the institution was supposed to be mild and paternal, but where by his account it was as rough and as brutal as any human relationship can be. He never knew who his father was, but it was assumed on the plantation that the father was white—probably his own master and owner.

In a sense, what Douglass has to say about his life in bondage is the old familiar material: there was a great deal of physical cruelty, hard work and bad food and poor living quarters, an eternal tormenting knowledge of illimitable insecurity, and worst of all a complete, taken-for-granted denial of the slave's right to be treated as a human being. He saw whippings and he experienced whippings, and before he reached his teens he learned that an overseer who administered cruel beatings but who did not seem to take personal delight in administering them was to be accounted a

**Narrative of the Life of Frederick Douglass, an American Slave, Written by Himself,** edited by Benjamin Quarles. The Harvard University Press. 163 pp. $3.50.

good and humane taskmaster. When he grew older and knew what words meant, he was able to write that the worst thing about being in bondage was "the dehumanizing character of slavery."

Fitzhugh, who after all was a white man, was able to write that the man who lost liberty and equality had lost "just nothing," but this man who had been born without the slightest chance to enjoy either would have contradicted him. He would have contradicted, indeed, every last item in the myth of the contented slave. He remarked, for instance, that slaves sang a great deal, and he had his comment on this fact:

I have often been utterly astonished, since I came to the north, to find persons who could speak of the singing, among slaves, as evidence of their contentment and happiness. It is impossible to conceive of a greater mistake. Slaves sing most when they are most unhappy. The songs of the slave represent the sorrows of his heart; and he is relieved by them, only as an aching heart is relieved by its tears. . . . I have often sung to drown my sorrow, but seldom to express my happiness. Crying for joy, and singing for joy, were alike uncommon to me while in the jaws of slavery.

Douglass' book is hard to read. It is written, to be sure, in unvarnished English prose, and there is nothing obscure or contrived about it, but it is still hard to read—simply because, more than one hundred years later, its account of the things men can do to those who are completely in their power is something to make the blood run cold. If there was a kindly, humane side to chattel slavery, this man who lived far outside of the cotton belt, who was for long periods a trusted house servant, who was even hired out (by his owner) to work in a shipyard, far from the eye of the man with the whip—this man, who should have seen that humane side if any slave could see it, never got a glimpse of it. "But for the hope of being free," Douglass wrote, "I have no doubt but that I should have killed myself."

In one way or another, while a pampered house servant in Baltimore, Douglass learned to read. He found books that discussed the problem of slavery and that told about what it was like to be free, and they made him all the more discontented—evidence of the practical wisdom of the cynical laws which made it illegal to teach any slave how to read and write. His condition, he felt, was worse after he became literate than it was before. Now he knew what he was missing; he had been taught, however imperfectly, to use his mind and to examine the thoughts of more fortunate men who had been able to use their minds to better advantage; and he put all of his anguish into the statement that this intensified all of his sufferings—"Anything, no matter what, to get rid of thinking!"

Douglass finally made his escape. His book, to repeat, was published in 1845, and it is significant that he does not tell how he escaped, or who helped him, or what the mechanics of the business were—he might get somebody into trouble if he explained things, or at the very least he might make it harder for the next man to get away. Even when he lived in the North, a free man working for wages, enjoying a life of his own, the shadow hung over him. He could not draw a really easy breath until after the sun went down at Appomattox.

Possibly Fitzhugh was the prophet of the future: there are millions of people alive today who live in very much the sort of intelligently contrived bondage which struck this excellent propagandist as the proper way to organize human society. But Fitzhugh's word has to go side by side with the word of Frederick Douglass, and this word from a man born under the lash is something to remember. Our generation might do much worse than to recall that America has bred men to whom liberty, however imperfect it might be and however hard it might be to come by, was quite literally worth dying for.

## What Welles Really Said

Gideon Welles came out of a very different stratum than either Fitzhugh or Douglass. He was a Connecticut Yankee, a one-time Democrat who turned Republican during the great ferment of the 1850's, and he became Lincoln's Secretary of the Navy, in which capacity he kept a diary which has been a source book for Civil War historians ever since; and the immense value of Welles's diary has always been the fact that he saw what he wrote about and that he wrote with objective exactitude.

Or—did he? The original manuscript of his diary is in the Library of Congress. It was brought to publication in 1911, and an examination of the manuscript indicates that certain changes were made between the time the old Yankee put pen to paper and the time when the business finally appeared in print. How reliable is this diary, anyway? Was it edited so as to bring later knowledge and riper judgments into play, or can it stand as a faithful, trustworthy account of what one man saw of the things that happened after Fitzhugh and Douglass had had their own say?

Civil War historiography has needed nothing much more than a new edition of the Welles diary, with scholarly editing to show precisely what he wrote at the time and what he put in later when he began to reflect that what he had written was going to be an essential part of American history. This new edition is now at hand. Howard K. Beale has edited the three-volume work, going over the original manuscript with painstaking care, writing a preface that shows when and why the revisions were undertaken, and presenting the whole with notes that show the reader exactly what Welles wrote at the time and what he wrote in later years. This new edition of *The Diary of Gideon Welles* is something every Civil War scholar will want.

It is also something that the general reader can enjoy, for Welles was a good diarist. He had a waspish way about him, he gave way to certain prejudices, and he presented his contemporaries and fellow workers as he saw them, writing, in the process, one of the great books about the Civil War years and the years immediately thereafter. No one has given as graphic or as readable a picture of the Civil War period.

Readable as it is, however, it is necessary to know how many of these day-by-day accounts were actually set down at the time and how many of them were fixed a decade later to make them fit in with what Welles and everyone else then knew. The answer, as Mr. Beale has found it—and no one will need to do this particular job over again—is that Welles was fairly human. He could go back, later on, to make a comment look more perceptive, to give himself credit for a little more foresight than he could have had at the time, to touch up a characterization in the light of knowledge that came long after. His diary, as originally published, was in fact rather substantially revised—partly by Welles himself, and partly by his son Edgar, who went over it with John Morse, who wrote the introduction, and toned down certain parts that might have led to unpleasantness or, possibly, to libel actions. Welles, for instance, was opposed to strong

---

**The Diary of Gideon Welles,** edited, previous errors corrected, and with an introduction by Howard K. Beale. W. W. Norton and Co. 3 volumes, boxed. $28.50.

---

drink, and when he saw statesmen or generals tipping the glass, and showing the effect, he wrote about it; most of which entries dropped out by the time the diary got into print. During the war Welles got a favorable impression of Grant, but he felt differently a bit later, and wrote that the general was "a wicked and bad man," that he was "deceptive, cunning, ambitious and unreliable," and that he had "low and vulgar instincts and tastes." These comments vanished before publication date.

Now the thing can be seen as Welles originally wrote it, and it is possible to see what Welles himself added or changed in later years and what his literary executors and editors changed after he himself was gone. As source material for the historian, the text is at last set as straight as anything of this kind can be. Its interest for the general reader is enhanced at the same time.

All of which leaves Welles, as a diarist, precisely where? At the conclusion of his exhaustive preface, Mr. Beale sums it up:

Because Gideon Welles was accurate, fair-minded, and cool-tempered to an extent marvelous in his day, this diary is valuable beyond most diaries. Even after his later emendations are eliminated, Welles remains a remarkable judge of men, and the prognostications that he did make before he began revising leave him a man of surprisingly prophetic insights. As a judge of men and an observer of passing events, Welles is surpassed by few chroniclers.

*An American Comment on the Grand Tour, 1873*